Passing the Torch Without Getting Scorched

Preserving Your Legacy With
Smart Succession Planning

LAWRENCE M. GOLD

authorHOUSE®

AuthorHouse™
1663 Liberty Drive
Bloomington, IN 47403
www.authorhouse.com
Phone: 1-800-839-8640

Published by AuthorHouse 8/13/2013

ISBN: 978-1-4918-0421-6 (sc)
ISBN: 978-1-4918-0398-1 (hc)
ISBN: 978-1-4918-0397-4 (e)

Library of Congress Control Number: 2013913575

Acknowledgement

Any book is a labor of lots of love and some pain. No writer can get through that process alone. In addition to my many colleagues, partners and friends who have helped me along the way, I could not have finished this journey without the love and support of my wife, Margo, and our three children, their spouses and our two grandchildren. They are my succession plan and they give me hope and support each and every day. Many thanks and much appreciation to all of you.

Lawrence M. Gold
August 13, 2013

Table of Contents

Introduction ix

Part I: The Basics of Succession Planning.......................... 1

Chapter 1 – Two People Walk into a Conference Room 3

Chapter 2 – Peeling Away the Myths and Mystery 11

Chapter 3 – Let's Get Started 18

Chapter 4 – Owners and Managers 23

Chapter 5 – Five Big Mistakes 26

Part II: Elements of Smart Succession Planning.................. 31

Chapter 6 – Ownership Succession..................................... 33

Chapter 7 – Management Succession 37

Chapter 8 – Valuations—Why They are So Important........... 41

Chapter 9 – Ownership Succession—Giving it Away............. 47

Chapter 10 – Ownership Succession—Selling It 56

Chapter 11 – Assessing Family Members and Management..............62

Chapter 12 – Sales of Equity to Third Parties and Employees............ 73

Chapter 13 – Shareholder Agreements 89

Chapter 14 – Stock Awards; Deferred Compensation 97

Chapter 15 – Bringing it all Together 101

Chapter 16 – We Now Return to Our Six Scenarios............ 105

Chapter 17 – Where Do I Go From Here?........................... 108

Owner Questionnaire Regarding Succession Planning.................. 111

Introduction

I started thinking about writing a book on the subject of succession planning some time ago as I was advising several clients about it. I realized it was an uncomfortable subject for most of them, and I started to wonder why. After all, this is a topic that any business owner should care deeply about. It affects the very survivability and continuity of the enterprise. Ownership of a business is typically the largest and most valuable asset any person can have. Yet, succession planning is shunted off to no man's land.

How often have you heard it said that a business owner treats his company like one of his or her own children?[1] Yet, when it comes to dealing with the critical issues of transferring ownership, much less management succession, it becomes a topic that virtually all business owners shy away from—almost as if they are afraid they will become infected with a deadly virus. Why is that so?

As I mulled this over, I concluded that the primary reason most business owners don't want to talk about succession planning—much less actually deal with the subject—is *fear*. To some extent, owners fear dealing with succession planning because they think it requires them to confront their own mortality. However true that may be, it doesn't fully answer the question. Another facet of the succession-planning

---

[1] This is the only footnote, so don't worry that you will be inundated with citations or cross-references. For ease of reading and writing, I will adopt the convention of using the masculine pronoun to refer to both genders. This is not out of any desire to discriminate in favor of or against the opposite gender. It's just easier. So, if this offends you, please accept my apologies and I hope you will read on.

conundrum involves the fact that succession planning appears to be so complex and multi-faceted, business owners just don't want to take the time to grapple with it. Since they see it as too complex, they avoid it, often precipitating the very complexities that careful planning could have avoided.

My purpose in writing this book is to dispel the many myths and fears that surround succession planning and to offer guidance and a more holistic approach to the subject—so that more business owners will realize that this just another set of strategic decisions they need to make and that they can do so with confidence and optimism.

This book is primarily designed for owners of family-owned or privately-owned businesses. These are the people who are most directly impacted by the need for, and the lack of, effective succession planning and who are most vulnerable if succession planning is not part of a solid business strategy. Part I is aimed at this audience and it attempts to whet the reader's appetite for more information and discussion about some of the specifics of succession planning.

Another part of this audience is senior management of these same businesses. While senior managers do not generally bring up the subject of succession planning, they are the ones whose lives and livelihoods will be impacted by it and who should therefore play a significant role in the formation and implementation of a succession plan. If they are truly part of a management team, then the lessons in this book will hopefully allow them to discuss the topic and deal with the subject with the owner.

Part II is designed to provide more details about the range of topics that fall within the ambit of succession planning. It is intended not only for business owners, but also for business advisors, financial planners, and others who may be more familiar with the basic concepts of succession planning but may not have thought about the topic in a comprehensive way.

Publicly-owned companies or institutionally-managed companies will typically have already dealt with succession planning—some more successfully than others. Board members and senior management of publicly-owned companies may benefit from the concepts described in this book, but they are not the primary audience for which it is intended.

I make a distinction in this book between succession planning and *effective* succession planning. If this book succeeds at all, I hope it's because I have placed more emphasis on the effectiveness of a succession plan rather than simply describing something that sits on a shelf in some office and never sees the light of day. In today's vernacular, such a plan is a "vampire" plan that functions, if at all, only in the dark—and can suck the blood out of any business.

If a business owner thinks in terms of leaving a lasting legacy rather than simply concocting some complicated plan, then I think he will better appreciate the importance and value of the effort to create an effective succession plan. That's what this book is all about. In the last analysis, the only true measure of success for an effective succession plan is the creation of a strong foundation for an owner's lasting legacy—whether for his family, his employees (or both), or for his community and his constituents who have been such a large part of his own success—his vendors, customers, and suppliers.

Also, permit me one disclaimer that any lawyer writing a book will appreciate. The components of an effective succession plan involve significant legal, tax, and accounting issues that no one book can cover in detail. This book is designed to give an owner or his management an overview of succession planning and some of its more important elements. This book is not a "how to" book, nor is it *Business Succession Planning for Dummies* [add copyright]. So, if you find that this book is helpful, please discuss it with your families and your advisors. Ultimately, they will be your best sources for information and guidance.

Part I

The Basics of Succession Planning

The universe is full of magic things, patiently waiting for our senses to grow sharper.
—Eden Phillpotts—A Shadow Passes

Simple terms often defy simple explanations. So it is with *succession planning*. While the subject of succession planning may appear self-evident on the surface—how to plan for succession in a business—it is not quite as easy as that to explain. The primary reason for this is that the subject of succession planning involves many disparate facets and many (if not all) of them are interrelated. Dealing with succession planning effectively is like peeling an artichoke. As one strips away each piece, one finds another piece underneath, and on and on until one arrives at the heart of the artichoke. The heart of our artichoke will be a structure for the elements of an effective succession plan, but before I get to the specifics of that plan, some basic overview is necessary.

Initially, I want to give you, the reader, not only an overview of succession planning with a taste of each layer, but also some tastes of the more basic concepts. In Part II, I describe many of these layers in greater detail and—hopefully, by the end—I tie them together so the reader will appreciate and understand the holistic approach that I so strongly advocate.

Whoever said that a picture is worth a thousand words knew what he was talking about. So to begin our journey, let's start with some examples of when and how a business owner might want to start thinking about succession planning.

Chapter 1

Two People Walk into a Conference Room

The moment you doubt whether you can fly, you cease for ever to be able to do it.
—J.M. Barrie, *Peter Pan*

The stage is set. Dim the lights. Cue the actors.

Scenario One:

John W. Owner calls his prospective son-in-law, Albert, into the conference room at his company's headquarters for a chat. General Equipment Manufacturing (GFM) makes and sells conveyor systems and was established by John's great-grandfather in 1897. It has been family-owned and family-managed ever since, but now John is getting older. He's sixty-seven and in good health. He and his wife, Marissa, have one child, Rebecca, who is twenty-two and is engaged to Albert. Their wedding is three weeks away.

Albert is a fine young man who recently graduated with an MBA from a nationally known business school, but he has no business experience. His father and grandfather are lawyers and his mother is a social worker.

John has already offered Albert a job with GEM as a sales assistant.

Albert thinks that John wants to go over some of the wedding plans. But John looks very serious and his brow is knitted with concern. The big smile on Albert's face suddenly disappears as John begins to talk.

Scenario Two:

In a variation of the first scenario, we still have GEM and John, but in this version there is no Albert. John wants to talk to Rebecca about her future. Rebecca is in her senior year at a well-known liberal arts college and is considering taking a year off after college to tour the world with her friend, Emily. She is majoring in philosophy.

Rebecca sits down in the conference room across from John and looks expectantly at her father as he begins to speak.

Scenario Three:

This time we still have GEM and John, but there is no Rebecca. John has had a very successful career in building GEM, but he and Marissa were not blessed with children of their own. The company has been John's surrogate child. He has raised it, nurtured it, and presided over its growth. GEM today is double the size it was when John took over as CEO from his father, Jeremy, twenty years ago. John is getting restless and wants other challenges in his life.

John has worked very hard to build a strong management team. He has a CFO, Elliott Spencer, who has been with him for fifteen years. His national sales manager, William First, has been with GEM for ten years. The VP of Manufacturing, Paul Burke, has been with GEM for seven years. Jillian Stewart, VP of Marketing, has been with GEM for five years. In addition to these four senior officers, John has brought in strong middle management. He has assembled a team of seven additional key personnel who are in sales, human relations, marketing, and manufacturing.

John has called for a meeting with his senior management team. They usually meet every Monday morning to go over plans for the week ahead. But this is Friday afternoon and they are all curious what's on John's mind. They begin to fidget and squirm as John starts to talk.

Scenario Four:

In yet another version, John still runs GEM and has the same management team. Rebecca is once more engaged to Albert. But this time John isn't the one who initiates a discussion about succession. Elliott Spencer, CFO, and Paul Burke, VP of Manufacturing, are having a cup of coffee one Thursday afternoon. They've worked closely together over the years and trust each other implicitly. Lately, they've seen hints that John is starting to slow down, and from offhand comments they've heard him make, they think he may be considering stepping down or even selling GEM. They have no idea about what role Albert may play. Elliott and Paul start to think about what might happen if John decides to leave, much less sell the company. "Paul," Elliott says, as he looks down into his coffee cup, "Let me ask you something."

Scenario Five:

John and Marissa have three wonderful children who all graduated from college, and John is considering offering two of them, Biff and Bob, positions in the business. The third child, Adriana, is going to law school. John is mulling over what he should do about inserting Biff and Bob into jobs at the company and whether he should make provisions now for them to own stock. If so, what does he do about Adriana? So he calls a family conference for Sunday afternoon. He's not sure how to begin, so he starts to talk about his great-grandfather and how the business got started. Biff and Bob look bored, and Adriana could care less. John stops giving the family history and stands up, puts down his glass of wine, and starts to speak from his heart.

Scenario Six:

John has been building GEM over the years and is proud of his success. He's built a strong management team and has rewarded them generously with annual cash bonuses for their performance. He's been thinking about starting to make gifts of stock to his children—Rebecca, Biff, and Bob—but he just hasn't gotten around to meeting with his lawyer and his CPA. This morning John got a phone call from Charles Morrison, CEO of one of his competitors, Giganticom.com. Charles tells John that he's prepared to buy GEM for a price that John never thought he would ever get for his company. The amount staggers him. *Gosh*, he thinks. *This is great. Now I can get some equity to my family and my key employees and they can all share in this great opportunity.* Suddenly, he begins to wonder if he has time to do that now. He picks up the phone to call his lawyer.

Stage Manager's Notes

These scenarios, or versions of them, play out every day in America. For every Facebook, Google, or General Electric, there are literally thousands of privately-owned businesses that are constantly wrestling with the issues of transferring wealth, finding and retaining qualified personnel, and looking to forge an exit strategy for existing owners. All of these issues are part of the fabric of *succession planning*. As we will see, succession planning involves a great deal more than simply designating an heir apparent for the business. For a succession plan to have any true merit and to really be effective, it must incorporate solutions for all of these subjects.

You should also note that although each of these scenarios is different, there are a number of common threads that run through all of them.

First, John has not created or implemented any kind of succession plan. His legacy, such as it is, lies firmly (or not so firmly) in his mind. Nothing has been translated into action. As it stands, no one but John has any clue yet as to what type of ownership or management transition John may have in mind.

Second, in all of these scenarios, there is an undercurrent of uncertainty and anxiety among the people who have a stake in the business about what the future may hold for them.

Third, whatever John is about to say to Albert, Rebecca, his management team, or his family, it's going to be something that will change their lives and their relationship with John.

Fourth, while it may seem obvious that the people to whom John is about to speak are nervous, it may not seem as obvious (but it is no less true) that John is nervous, too.

Fifth, John is not operating in a vacuum, and just as he is having thoughts about succession, so are his key people.

Sixth, time is not John's best friend right now. The longer he procrastinates—something tells him—the harder this is going to get.

We won't go further with these examples right now, but we will come back to them later to see how these meetings might have fared and how different the circumstances might have been had John created an effective succession plan.

One question should immediately come to mind as you begin to think about these scenarios or others that may have popped into your head. Why would any successful businessman not do something about this? Why would someone who has navigated the shoals of treacherous competitors, endured volatile markets, and experienced the highs and lows of business *not* prepare his family, his company, his employees and his customers for what will be an inevitable event—later if not sooner? By *inevitable* I don't just mean death or some other catastrophic event. By inevitable, I mean the evolutionary arc of any enterprise as it develops from an entrepreneurial start-up to an institutionally managed, if not owned, business.

If these scenarios paint a fairly typical picture of different ways that the need for succession planning becomes apparent, and if they are prototypical of life in the privately-owned company world, then—to ask the question we did before but somewhat differently—*why on earth are business owners so loath to come to grips with it?*

There are many reasons that otherwise sane and rational people avoid this topic like the plague.

First, for an owner to be willing to consider succession, he must confront his own mortality. While death may not be the only reason a successor is needed, it is the reason that first comes to most people's minds. Let's face it; death is a scary subject. It's the same reason that many people put off writing their wills or purchasing life insurance. One likes to think (even if he knows otherwise) that he will live to a ripe old age, surrounded by doting family members who wait patiently and breathlessly for the patriarch to award the birthright to a loyal and devoted child as he prepares to shuffle off this mortal coil. Others may take a more cynical and stoic attitude and feel that, since they came up the hard way, let their survivors deal with the problem. It won't matter to the current owner, who will by then be beyond caring.

It is not easy for someone to contemplate what will happen after he is gone, much less deal with the issues that this unhappy event will precipitate. And so one procrastinates and delays and delays and delays. Perhaps the owner thinks that natural selection will occur and a successor will emerge from the current lot of contenders. Perhaps a white knight will come along—someone who embodies all the fine qualities that the owner finds so sorely lacking in his current crop of descendants or managers. Perhaps a buyer for the company will surface and rescue him from these difficult decisions. There are so many possibilities to hope for. But, as one wise man once said, "Hope is not a strategy."

There are more reasons, though, why owners avoid the subject of succession planning. A successful and dynamic owner typically believes with all his heart that he can still run his business better than anyone else. He's not ready to retire or transfer control to anyone else. He's not even willing to think about grooming someone for that task.

Moreover, whether or not he has been blessed with children of his own, he has treated his business as his child, in some cases like a lover. He has devoted his energy and mental and physical strengths to nurturing and supporting this enterprise and he has sacrificed many things—particularly *time*—so that his business would grow and prosper. To even think about letting that go and surrendering his beloved company to someone else—much less to a stranger—is more than unsettling; it's downright unthinkable.

There's more. Given the dynamics of human relationships, an owner believes that if he brings up the subject of succession—and actually does something about it—he is bound to alienate one or more of his trusted family members or key employees. How can he anoint a successor, much less plan for that eventuality, without running the serious risk of losing some key people on whom he has depended—or alienating one or more members of his family? He may also think: *since retirement is so far off and I'm in excellent health, why stir the pot now?*

Finally, if an owner begins to think about succession, he soon realizes that it is a multifaceted, complex subject. There are so many variables and issues to consider. How does one even know where to start? Also, he may need to contend with certain pressing issues on a daily basis: disgruntled employees, unhappy customers, recalcitrant suppliers, fierce competitors, a new kitchen, or a nasty slice in his golf game. Why tackle something as difficult, daunting, and seemingly unpleasant as succession planning?

The truth is that the subject of succession planning is more often than not left untouched and ignored until it is too late. Succession planning is avoided like the plague because a business owner often feels (even if he won't say so) that if he starts to deal with it, he will catch some dreaded disease (not necessarily the plague) and bring about sooner rather than later the very consequence that a succession plan prescribes—his own demise.

From the employee's perspective, while there may be a sense of urgency or discomfort over the lack of a succession plan, there is also the ambivalent sense that—as long as no succession plan exists—every employee still has a chance to catch the brass ring. However, the lack of a plan fosters (unintentionally or not), a competitive environment which, to some owners, may seem productive. However, if one examines this more closely, one sees how corrosive this internal competition can be. It doesn't take a psychologist or human resources expert to understand that when two or more people are vying for attention—if not for the highest rung on the ladder—competition will inevitably dampen or destroy any sense of collaboration or common purpose. It will also set good people against each other, often with unintended and awful consequences.

So, let's take a look at this subject and examine what makes an effective succession plan. In doing so, perhaps I can remove the mystery and the myths about it and let sunshine in on this virtually unexplored corner of the business world.

First, I will describe some of the more common myths and mysteries that persist about succession planning.

Chapter 2

Peeling Away the Myths and Mystery

I love it when a plan comes together.
—Colonel John "Hannibal" Smith
(George Peppard) in *The A-Team*

Before I get into the nuts and bolts of succession planning, I want to dispel the most common misconceptions and myths about it. Also, I will try to eliminate some of the mystery about what succession planning is—and what it is not.

Let's first talk about the myths.

Myth One: My life is over.

The first myth about succession planning is that it is an "end of life" decision. Many people believe that if they start to think about succession planning they are, in effect, foreshadowing their own demise—or, if not their actual demise, then at least the beginning of a downward spiral toward it. This is just not so. First, as I have already pointed out and will talk more about later, succession planning is very much a part of a living, dynamic business process. It can and should be a liberating experience, not a painful or threatening one. To a large extent, much of the attitude toward succession planning depends on the owner's perspective and attitude. If he believes he is setting the groundwork for the next level of growth for his company and, furthermore, that he is establishing a sound foundation for his family's future, then he will approach the subject with enthusiasm. On the other hand, if he believes that he is opening the door for his imminent departure from the company, he will either not proceed or will do so with great reluctance.

Myth two: It's too difficult.

The second myth is that succession planning is just too difficult to understand and too hard to deal with. One of the most persistent impressions about succession planning is that it is too complex and cumbersome. It requires an owner to consider subjects about which he may be ignorant or ill-informed. Consequently, most owners don't want to deal with it—especially if the business is running smoothly, profits are up, customers are growing and expanding, and morale is high. And if the business is having problems, especially financial ones, then succession planning is the last thing an owner wants to think about. He's dealing with survival.

It is simply not true that the subject of succession planning is too difficult to understand. Nor does it have to be overly complex. In its basic terms, an effective succession plan is another business strategy. It is no different in its basic form from any other business strategy that deals with entering new markets, targeting new customers, providing incentives to employees, or deciding what new equipment to buy or lease. When an owner makes those decisions, he relies on good advice, especially his own. He makes a calculation of the risks and rewards of allocating business resources to a new project; he tries to figure out whether the return on that investment is sufficiently assured—or, conversely, whether the risk to the business of *not* making that investment is too high to warrant moving forward.

So it is with succession planning. If one breaks the process down into digestible components and deals with them separately—and then brings those components together into a holistic, systematic process—then the often-perceived complexities break down into quite understandable and manageable pieces.

Also, the criteria for evaluating a succession plan are really no different from those for any other business decision. The owner takes stock of his circumstances and of his business and decides what kind of return he can get on his investment in his people. And the return on that investment is not only for the benefit of the owner but also for his family—and his key employees and *their* families—

Will a succession plan guarantee future success or growth? Of course not, but neither will the purchase of a newer and faster machine—unless there are orders for the goods that machine will produce, making it a necessity.

If it is true, and I think it is, that any business that wants to grow and produce more profits in the future needs a strategic plan to help achieve those results, then it is also true that one key element of any strategic business plan is the matter of succession.

Myth Three: My key people will leave me.

A third myth about succession planning is that it can lead to defections by key employees and it can demoralize them.

As I try to emphasize in this book, an effective succession plan can actually prevent defections and instill even higher morale among all employees—especially key employees.

Why is this so? There are several reasons. First, an effective succession plan gives everyone comfort that the owner has thought about the future and has created a plan to assure the company's continued survival and chances for growth. That alone has to make both family members and employees feel good.

Second, as I discuss more thoroughly in a later chapter, there are many distinctions between ownership succession and management succession. Separate considerations affect each of these aspects of succession planning, but as far as key employees are concerned, the latter is far more important to them. Sure, key people would like to be able to earn a share of ownership, and with the right kind of succession plan, they certainly can. However, ownership is not as important to most key employees as making sure that an effective management team is in place to run the business profitably and strategically. Think of working in a building with a leaky roof. No one wants to sit there all day and have water dripping on his head. Getting the roof fixed will make the entire organization feel better and work better. Well, an effective succession plan fixes that leaky roof.

Thirdly, while it is possible that putting together a succession plan and identifying a business successor (owner or manager) may cause certain key people to look around for another position, that won't necessarily happen. In fact, the opposite can occur just as easily. If the owner has done a good job of providing meaningful incentives for key personnel and has instilled in his management team a true sense of teamwork and collaboration, then the fact that Bill has been selected over John or Jane doesn't necessarily mean that John or Jane will leave the company. John and Jane may feel that they are just as capable as Bill and that if they stick around, they can prove that to the owner and he will change his mind—or they may feel that Bill is a good choice and they are happy to stay and work with him. The larger the organization, the more likely this more placid acceptance of a succession plan will be. Even in smaller companies, if the succession plan is comprehensive and offers meaningful incentives—for ownership or bonuses, or both—then loss of key people is by no means a foregone conclusion.

Even if this more hopeful view of succession planning does not materialize and one or more key persons leave—that may end up being the best result for the business anyway. After all, if loyalty is a key factor in evaluating key employees (and I think it is), then a key person who chucks it in because he or she wasn't selected has a pretty underdeveloped sense of loyalty, and it's better to know that now rather than later.

Myth Four: It won't work.

A fourth myth about succession planning is that it doesn't work. An owner goes to the trouble and expense of creating a rock solid, gold-plated succession plan and then it just founders and gathers dust and no one pays any attention to it.

This is probably the most pernicious of all the myths about succession planning. It is undeniably true that many succession plans fail, but the fault, dear Brutus, is not in the stars. Usually the finger of failure points right back to the owner. Typically, an owner will start a process toward developing a good succession plan and then abandon the effort. He either gets distracted by other business matters, or he can't make up his mind, or he gets tired of hearing how complex it can be. Whatever the reason, what started out as an exciting project for the owner and his managers turns into a nightmare. Both the owner and his key people are disappointed and demoralized; morale, which had been high, plummets to new depths. Even worse, after a succession plan is put in place, the owner may decide that he made a mistake. It's not what he wants to see happen. Rather than calling in his family members or his management team, however, he just unilaterally abandons the plan. He does have that right, but at what cost?

Also, succession plans can become so complex and cumbersome that they simply fall due to their own weight. It's as if gravity pulls them down with a jarring thud.

Finally, succession plans, like any other component of a business plan, must be dynamic, flexible, and able to adapt to new circumstances. This means that an owner must periodically review the plan and modify it to conform to changing circumstances. If the plan sits on a shelf or in a safe and gathers dust, then it will inevitably fail. Indeed, one of my suggestions is that the owner not just review it himself, but actually meet with his key personnel to go over the plan, get input from them and then revise it as he thinks appropriate.

Myth Five: It is a consultant's and a lawyer's annuity.

A fifth myth is that succession plans are the creations of business consultants, lawyers, accountants, and other advisors who are just looking for more fees. In my experience, nothing is further from the truth. In fact, discussing succession planning with a business owner is one of the few times that an advisor can encourage action before a critical event occurs. So often the advisors get called in after the fact. There's a dispute with a customer over a contract. The lawsuit that the owner has dreaded and been avoiding has been filed. The merger letter of intent has already been signed. These are the times when the owner thinks of calling his advisors and it's usually late in the day.

With succession planning, much like estate planning, the advisors have the opportunity to prepare for an outcome that has not yet occurred—and most often at far less cost than would be incurred without planning.

So much for the most common myths about succession planning. How about the mysteries?

In most cases, the mysteries about succession planning are tied to the myths I've already identified. It's too complex. It doesn't work. Most of them fail. It's just a scheme by money-hungry professionals. If I can slice through the web of myths, I believe I can remove much of the mystery at the same time.

In addition, many of the components of an effective succession plan are driven by legal, accounting, and tax considerations, and some of them may seem very esoteric and complex. Most owners don't understand—and don't even want to understand—these concepts or issues. They would rather depend on their advisors to guide them. When it comes to transferring ownership or management of their businesses, however, they want to understand; they need to understand. It therefore becomes necessary for them to gain some appreciation of these issues. That takes time and it takes patience on the part of the advisors. If you have ever sat with a lawyer or accountant and tried to understand some of the nuances of a deferred compensation plan, you know exactly what I mean.

Also, because there are many components to a succession plan—as I will show—there are many moving parts and it sometimes may seem impossible to bring them all together into a cohesive, comprehensive, and understandable whole. It's as if there must be some secret sauce that must be added to the mix to make it "cook." In reality, there is no secret sauce or magic bullet, and the really effective succession plans perform the feat of bringing the components together in a smooth, holistic pattern that may seem like magic, but it's not.

As I go through the various steps of formulating and then implementing an effective succession plan, I will shed as much light as possible on these so-called mysteries and will try to dispel the myths. I will also try to make clear that when succession planning is broken down into simple, understandable steps, a succession plan can truly be a liberating and invaluable business tool.

Chapter 3

Let's Get Started

Whatever you can do, or dream you can do, begin it.
Boldness has genius, power and magic in it. Begin it now.
—Johann Wolfgang von Goethe

What's a Succession Plan?

Often I will pick up a book or start to read an article about a subject and before I get past the first paragraph, I'm told that before I can learn about that subject, what I really need to do is something entirely different. I call this approach the advisor's two-step. It's not really a bait and switch and I have no quarrel with being thorough—but it can be hugely frustrating to think that I'm about to learn something about a topic (succession planning, for example) only to be told right away that before I get to that, I must first do something else. For example, *review my company's strategic plan* or *go through an assessment of the strengths and weaknesses of management.* It really gets me upset and I start to grind my teeth.

So, this book will not do that. I will start with succession planning and I will end with succession planning. There are a number of important topics to address when considering this subject, but I will try to stay focused on succession planning and nothing else.

I won't belabor the need for preparation or self-examination. Of course those subjects are important. I believe, however, that if I remain rigorous about trying to explain what makes an effective succession plan and how an owner can inject vitality into the process, then the rest will naturally follow.

So to begin, I want to start by explaining what a succession plan is and what it is not and what makes any succession plan—however it may be structured—an *effective* succession plan.

In its simplest terms, a succession plan provides a path for transition of ownership or management, or both, of a business enterprise. That's it. Many bells and whistles can be added to this simple concept, but I want to keep reminding you that this is what a succession plan ultimately is. If I can keep you focused on that simple construct, then I believe you can avoid much of the confusion and obfuscation that typically surrounds the process of putting a succession plan together.

Ownership Succession and Management Succession—Two Very Different Concepts

Keep in mind the distinction that I've made between ownership succession and management succession. Ownership transition is very different from management transition. The two require different strategies and approaches. Often when one talks about succession planning, however, these two very different concepts are lumped together as if they are fungible. They are most definitely not.

Here is an easy example. The owner of a business has three children, all of whom are out of college or graduate school and active in the business—yet none of them own any portion of the business. Having met with his estate lawyer and accountant, the owner may decide to start giving stock to his children, or he may set up some trusts or limited liability companies (LLCs) to own stock. He's been advised to get assets out of his estate for estate tax purposes and so he begins to do so. Later we will examine some of the pitfalls of this strategy, but from the owner's perspective, he's doing two things. He's removing appreciated assets from his estate (he hopes) and transferring some percentage of ownership to his children, either directly or indirectly. Not a bad succession plan, right? What's wrong with this picture?

A number of things are wrong with this picture. Has enough thought been given to what happens to the rest of the owner's stock? Is it really outside of his estate for tax purposes? What about the management team? Will they be left out in the cold when the owner dies? What if the children don't agree what to do? (Imagine such a thing!) Worse, what happens if one or more of the children gets divorced or moves to India to meditate? What happens to the stock then? What happens if one of the children wants to buy out the others? Or one of the children wants to sell his stock? Is a mechanism in place to provide for any of these contingencies?

More important than any of these questions, though, is the question that arises when one realizes that so far, all the owner has done is provide for transition of some ownership. He's done nothing on the equally critical issue of management succession. If he doesn't also deal with this subject, he and his children are liable to end up with stock that is worthless—or at least worth far less than what he had hoped.

The converse is also true. If an owner who owns 100 percent of his business decides to make arrangements for management transition through a selection process that ensures continued successful management of the business—but he doesn't deal with the issue of ownership succession—then he hasn't accomplished an effective succession plan. All he's really done is set up a no-win situation between his family and his management when he dies.

Blending the Two Together

The first critical point to recognize is that an *effective* succession plan deals with both types of transition—ownership transition and management transition. That is what I mean by using the term *holistic*. A holistic succession plan blends the best parts of ownership succession and management succession and creates a symbiotic relationship between the two elements. This makes it possible for future owners—be they family members, key employees, or third parties—to have a positive, forward-thinking attitude and relationship with the management team and vice versa. Is this easy? No. Is it attainable? Yes. In order to achieve this nirvana of succession, an owner has to understand that he's going to have to deal with each element separately and with different criteria and goals.

Before going further with the structure and components of an effective succession plan, let's make sure we also know what a succession plan is *not*. A succession plan is not a cure for management or ownership problems. A succession plan alone will not generate more revenues or profits. A succession plan will not increase the company's customer base and it will not stifle the company's competitors. A succession plan is not a cure for all company ailments.

Moreover, a succession plan is not a static, immovable, and immutable construct. A succession plan requires vigilance and periodic modification, or at least periodic review. We all know that circumstances change. Profitable businesses learn how to adapt and to adapt quickly to those changes. Succession plans are no different. The trick is not to change things too rapidly in response to what may be fads and not trends and not to discard solid pieces of a good succession plan because of what may be transitory and ephemeral blips.

Finally, a succession plan—or, I should say, an *effective* succession plan—is not an ultimatum delivered from on high by an imperious owner. It is the result of careful deliberation, consultation, and coordination with other aspects of a strategic plan for the business. Thus, a succession plan derives its power and usefulness from the breadth of its reach and the ways it tries to satisfy myriad conditions and circumstances.

From a family perspective, a succession plan will not resolve the issues that cause family members to quarrel with one another. Nor will a succession plan effectively deal with a dipsomaniacal nephew or slow-witted cousin. A succession plan cannot be extrapolated into a cure for all family ills.

A truly effective succession plan is more like a symphony, with many moving parts and a conductor to guide its sound, its harmonies, and its resonance.

I provide a questionnaire in an appendix for business owners to get acquainted with some of the issues they will face as they begin to think about succession planning. This questionnaire is not designed to be all-inclusive. It does not ask all the questions that arise when one begins to consider creating a succession plan. What this questionnaire *will* do is provide some guidance and insight that can get you started. You're welcome to take a look at the questionnaire at any time, but I believe it will have more impact and be more effective if you wait until you've finished reading this book.

Chapter 4

Owners and Managers

*The reason I talk to myself is because
I'm the only one whose answers I accept.*
—George Carlin

Owners

In this chapter, I describe the differences between ownership succession and management succession in more detail. Understanding the differences between these two pillars of business organization is critical to any coherent, effective succession plan. Both of these elements involve decisions that affect people, their livelihood, and their families. A business owner knows this. If he forgets the scope and the impact of succession planning, then any succession plan is bound to fail. This concern is part of the reason that owners are reluctant to tackle the subject.

There is nothing more crucial to the success of any business than trying to maintain family harmony on the one hand, and keeping good people and maintaining the intellectual capital of an enterprise on the other. Owners tend to feel that if a solid, well-performing management team is already in place, then all a succession plan can do is mess up that team; complicating that picture with family considerations is like playing with fire.

This concern is real, but it is not well-founded. Succession concerns for family more often than not center around ownership issues. Who gets what percent of the equity and when? Will family members enjoy both governance rights—voting, and economic rights—distributions? Family members will be more concerned about how they, as owners, will relate to the principal owner—their father, or uncle, or grandfather. If the principal owner is a very domineering person, then many family members may well prefer to remain in the background, collect their quarterly checks, and stay quiet.

Family members, other than employees, tend not to worry too much about how the business is running or what business strategies should be employed. They focus on more personal issues.

Managers

For managers, the focus is very different. They do worry about business issues. They do worry about profits, customers, competitors, and growth. They see ownership as something that they can look forward to earning, not something that they will receive because they are members of the lucky sperm club. Managers are concerned about job security, compensation, and growing with the company.

Ownership succession invariably involves matters of family dynamics, family personalities, and family histories. Management succession may involve family issues, but typically does not. Of course, personality issues and history play a part, but they tend to be less personal. Blood remains thicker than water.

Ownership succession is generational. It deals with long-term transition and quasi-permanent—if not permanent—change. Management succession is inherently more transitory. No one expects a new CEO or CEO-to-be to last forever. Management succession accommodates change and continuous transition.

Finally, ownership succession deals with the basic fabric of the enterprise—the warp and woof of equity with its perennial issues of governance (who gets to vote?) and economic interest (who gets the money?) Management succession is more about exercising control of the business itself and driving the ship of state.

In both cases, the hopes and desires and skills and talents of people are fundamental, but they diverge, depending on which side of the fence they live on—the ownership side or the management side. Of course, in many cases, family members work for the company; in other cases, key management may already have equity interests in the company. So the lines can blur. It is useful, however, for the owner to treat them separately for purposes of creating a succession plan. Why? The goals of both groups may differ strategically. Yet, in order for a succession plan to work, both groups must be addressed, and solutions must be derived that satisfy both.

The fascinating thing about succession planning is that while there are many differences—crucial differences—between ownership succession and management succession, the truly *effective* succession plans blend both of them into a holistic system creating more balance, more synergy, and more chances for success.

Chapter 5

Five Big Mistakes

When I joined this firm as a brash young man
Well, I said to myself, "Now brash young man
Don't get any ideas."
Well I stuck to that,
And I haven't had one in years.
　　　　　—lyrics of "The Company Way" from
　　　　How to Succeed in Business Without Really Trying

The number, breadth, and intensity of the mistakes made in succession planning could serve as a book by itself. In almost every instance where a company struggles with succession—or fails to deal with it altogether—the stories that make the headlines are truly heartbreaking; we all tend to read those stories avidly but never believe that could happen to us. The truth is that it happens every single day. Just recently, *The New York Times* reported on a typical succession planning fiasco that befell the founding families of the *Archie* comic book publishing empire. The two founding families had a succession plan of sorts, but it devolved into allowing one child from each family to serve as co-CEOs. As might be predicted, they had a series of falling outs and disagreements over the future growth of the company. One wanted to keep the company intact, as it had been, while the other wanted to expand the business with capital from outside investors. When the bickering became really corrosive, a slew of lawsuits were filed; now both families are locked in a fight that shows no signs of becoming resolved. This is just one story. There are many, many more.

I have tried to collect the major mistakes that I've seen or read about that have occurred with ineffective succession planning. I've limited these to what I call the five major mistakes.

Mistake Number One—·No Plan

The number one mistake that an owner can make is to never make a succession plan. If he does not have a plan to effect orderly change, the owner risks leaving his company and the constituent elements of his company in chaos if and when something bad happens. This can affect his family, his employees, his vendors, his customers, and others who rely upon him and his business. Postponing the inevitability of change is a recipe for disaster. If an owner thinks that trying to put a succession plan together will create dissension or will exacerbate tension within his family or his company, think what will happen if he doesn't do anything at all to establish some orderly transition of ownership and management. Whatever dissension or tension might result from having a succession plan is dwarfed by the dissension and tension—not to mention the disruption and disorganization—that will ensue should the owner abruptly depart the scene and leave it to others to sort out.

Hopefully, the analysis and discussion in this book makes the prospect of creating a succession plan less formidable and less frightening. If that is the case, an owner should begin the process as soon as he can.

Mistake Number Two—Delay

The second biggest mistake is to postpone the decision to implement a succession plan until a specific need arises, such as the arrival of an unsolicited offer to purchase the company. The reason this is a big mistake is that it may be too late to do anything that will reduce the economic consequences of that transaction—specifically, the tax consequences. Why? It's because the value of the company has now been set by the new offer that's just been presented. Remember our fundamental definition of fair market value? It's what a willing buyer will pay and a willing seller will take. If a large offer arrives, then that pretty much sets the value. So an owner who has not created incentives for his management and who wants to do so may now find that the economic incentive has basically evaporated. Whatever type of incentive he wants to create will be valued at the proposed sale price and there is no immediate upside for his employees. Management incentives offer powerful retention possibilities, and management retention is usually a key point for any buyer of a business. So the issue goes beyond simply rewarding key employees. It deals with keeping them around to assure future success.

Also, if an owner has been planning to transfer equity to his family and a purchase offer has arrived, it's the same issue. Whatever he chooses to do, with whatever discounts on the equity value he may have been able to employ, all of that may now be much less effective because of the new offer. That new offer has established a value and it's going to be hard to disengage from it.

Timing is very important in most things and especially so here. The key take away from this discussion: Don't wait and don't delay.

Third Mistake—Fits and Starts

The third big mistake is to start to develop a succession plan and then stop. It's one thing if an owner has begun to think about a succession plan, but kills the idea before he has had any substantive discussions with his family or his management. It's very different if he has had those discussions and then abandons the idea. Whether he intended to do so or not, the fact is that the owner has raised expectations among those near and dear to him—family and employees. Not only are they going to be disappointed if the owner stops the process, but also they can become demoralized, disenchanted or disgruntled—or all three. One could say it's almost worse to start and then abandon the idea rather than never to have started the process. This doesn't mean that once an owner begins to develop a succession plan he is forever committed to it. It isn't an all or nothing proposition. However, if an owner *does* start to create a succession plan, he needs to give a good explanation to his family and his employees if he decides to pull the plug. If he gives them reasonable and rational bases for stopping before the plan is finalized, then he can buy time to complete the project. The most important thing is to be as transparent as possible with the key stakeholders and to try to help them understand what the owner is thinking.

Mistake Number Four—Do it and then Forget About It

The fourth big mistake is to believe that once an owner has gone through the difficulties and stress of creating a succession plan, he can let it alone and not bother with it anymore. Circumstances change: an owner's view of the world and of his company may change; the industry may change. For a succession plan to be effective, it must be flexible and adaptable. The owner must be able to reserve the right to change it as the current conditions warrant.

If the owner puts stock in a trust for his children, the trust must permit the trustee to alter some of the distribution or disposition provisions that take into account changes in circumstances. If the owner has established either an equity program or a deferred compensation program for key employees, he must reserve the right to change those plans if necessary. He may need to modify them to either limit or enlarge participation, or he may need to terminate the plans.

In addition to maintaining flexibility, the owner should periodically review his succession plan—including any equity or deferred compensation plans—so that he not only can see what changes may be required, but also so he can confirm and verify the components of the succession plan and make sure the plan is consistent with his goals and his intentions.

Mistake Number Five—Too Much Tinkering

The fifth big mistake is the opposite of mistake number four. The owner must resist the temptation to tinker too frequently with his succession plan. There will always be some unexpected consequences or unanticipated problems. If the plan has been carefully created and the owner is confident in what he has created, however, then he needs to let things settle in and the plan must be given time to "bake," so to speak. Inconsistency and frequent changes deprive a succession plan of one of its key goals: a sustainable and coherent plan for the future of the company and its ownership. Too many changes will create an environment of uncertainty and unease, not only among employees but also among family members. An owner should avoid this as much as possible. Consistency, continuity, and stability should be the watchwords for any effective succession plan.

Part II

Elements of

Smart Succession Planning

The advantages of a hereditary Monarch are self-evident. Without some such method of prescriptive, immediate and automatic succession, an interregnum intervenes, rival claimants arise, continuity is interrupted and the magic is lost.
—Harold Nicholson

Now that I've given you an overview of the basic concepts for effective succession planning, it is time to drill down into some of the specifics. As we have already seen, there are many components or elements to succession planning and there is no single template or form of succession planning for every business. Just as every business owner and every business is unique, so are the circumstances that may dictate which elements of a succession plan need to be incorporated which may be deferred, and which simply do not apply or will not work.

As you read the chapters in Part II, keep in mind that one or more of these strategies or programs may not work for you. Based on my experience, I believe that most of them will be appropriate for you to consider, if not adopt; however, I also know that you will not—and you should not—simply accept all of them as appropriate for you. That's fine and certainly understandable. My hope is that some of these ideas will resonate with you and that you will find them appealing. Also, keep in mind that with each of these components, there are many variations and alternatives. One size definitely does not fit all. It is my hope that the discussion of the elements I have highlighted will give you a proper grounding and set a solid foundation for you to review with your advisors and then adapt or modify them for your specific circumstances.

I'll begin by highlighting the distinction between ownership succession and management succession. As you will soon see, these concepts are not only very distinct, but also very different.

Chapter 6

Ownership Succession

Never put off until tomorrow what you can do
the day after tomorrow.

—Mark Twain

The crux of ownership succession lies in the way a business owner wants his family, his employees, or others to acquire ownership of the business. If the owner doesn't want his family to own the business, then the issue becomes one of finding the best way to provide equity to a potential successor who is not a family member—whether that person is an existing employee or a third party. As we will see, these two objectives are not mutually exclusive, and I use the term *equity* to describe the owner's interest. It may be stock, if the company is a corporation, or it may be membership interests, if the company is a limited liability company. Those are the two most common forms of entities. There are others, of course, such as limited partnerships and joint ventures, but whatever the type of entity, I will use the term *equity* to stand for the ownership interests which include two very fundamental pieces. First, there is the right to vote that equity (assuming that the equity has voting rights), and second, there are the economic rights to receive dividends, distributions, or other payments. For simplicity's sake, I will use the term *equity* to include both sets of rights or benefits.

Before discussing ownership succession, be it to family members or to others, let's try to simplify the basic issue. There are really only two ways the owner of a business can dispose of his equity. He can give it away or he can sell it. That's it. There are, of course, many variations on these two themes; creative lawyers, accountants, and business consultants have thought of many of them, with so many bells and whistles that one's head will swim just trying to understand them.

No matter how complex the nature of the owner's equity may be, the choices for disposition are very basic: gifts or sales. Keep that in mind as we embark on these discussions.

For the most part, the choice of gift or sale will be driven by two sets of competing issues. First, there are issues that relate to how much equity will be given away or sold and how much control the owner will retain. How much control is the owner willing to part with while he is still alive and active in the business? If he disposes of equity to his family or to other key personnel, what happens if they leave or become disenchanted with ownership? How can the owner protect himself from an ungrateful child or a disgruntled employee?

Second, there are tax issues to be considered. Estate tax considerations may dictate how to employ these strategies—or more precisely, how much to give away and how much to sell. Estate tax issues are not the only tax concerns, however. Other tax matters that invariably arise relate to recognition of taxable gain on a sale or the gift tax consequences of a gift.

More issues are involved than control and taxation. Once an owner has transferred equity to someone else, no matter how minimal it may be, there are constraints on the owner's ability to run the business with a free hand as he did before. Moreover, there are requirements that, at least for corporations, dividends, or other distributions, must be paid pro rata among all equity holders. This may pose limitations on how much or how little disposable cash an owner wants—or needs—to distribute. There are ways to adjust for these pro rata rules, but they involve adjusting compensation and that can be tricky and problematic.

Then, finally, there is the problem of what to do with gifts or sales of equity to family members who later get divorced, die, or just become disappointments. What happens to the equity? Will a philandering spouse end up with half of the equity in a divorce settlement or judgment? Does the owner really want his ten-year-old grandson to become an equity holder in the business? Can the owner "claw" back the equity somehow? If he does have that ability and he really tried to give the equity to his child in the first place, has he really even made a gift of the equity at all?

If the owner sells the equity, how will the recipient pay for it? Even adjusting for differences in valuation—which we will discuss separately—if the transaction is structured to qualify as a sale, it must in fact be a real sale. This means that the purchaser, whether he is a family member or key employee, must somehow pay for the equity with real dollars at some real point in time. This can be tricky and problematic as well.

This can happen during the owner's lifetime or upon his death and there are many variations on the basic theme. For example, an owner can arrange for a portion of his equity to be given to his spouse or his children during his lifetime, with the remainder going to them upon death. Alternatively, an owner can set up various trusts for the benefit of his spouse and his children and the equity can be put into these trusts for their benefit.

Another strategy is for an owner to sell his equity to family members during his lifetime, usually by taking back promissory notes for the purchase price. These can be paid over time, or upon the occurrence of a liquidity event, such as a sale of the company.

In order to minimize an owner's estate tax liability, a number of strategies are available to dispose of his equity while retaining elements of management control—and, hopefully, excluding the appreciation of that equity from the owner's estate.

The short version of this story is that the best succession plans—the most *effective* succession plans—employ a combination of ownership succession techniques, which we will explore in more depth. Suffice it to say, the main pitfall to avoid is *rigidity*. No ownership succession plan will be successful if it does not allow for adaptability to changes in circumstances, business conditions, family dynamics, and employee retention.

One of the most intricate balances that most owners want to strike in any of these situations is the balance between disposing of ownership and maintaining as much control over the governance and management of the company as possible.

With gifts or direct sales, this can be accomplished through taking back voting proxies for the equity; however, there is always an issue of whether the owner has effectively disposed of the equity if he retains too much control over the voting of that equity.

In the case of transfers to minimize estate taxes, there are several strategies that will allow an owner to retain control. For example, in a frequently used strategy known as an estate *freeze*, the owner will transfer his equity to a single-member LLC (of which he is the sole member) and then sell a significant portion of his LLC interests (but not more than 50%) to a trust established for his family. In this way, the owner retains control via the LLC in which he owns a controlling interest, while still disposing of a significant portion of LLC ownership to a trust through a sale—again based upon an independent valuation of the underlying asset in the LLC—namely, the equity in the company.

Chapter 7

Management Succession

*I'm not afraid of death; I just don't want to be there
when it happens.*

—Woody Allen

Now, let's discuss management succession.

An owner could decide that he wants his family to continue to own the business, but he may, at the same time, decide that no one in his family is capable of *running* the business. How does he deal with this conundrum? Conversely, an owner may feel that his oldest child, who has been working in the business for years, is perfectly capable of running the company, but what does he do about his protégé who has been a valuable and loyal employee for many years? What does he do about his other children, none of whom want to work in the business but who deserve to share in its growth and value as members of the family?

Each situation is unique and there is no magic answer or formula that will solve or resolve all of these issues. But an owner must consider these issues separate and apart from the ownership succession issues, because if he does not, he is more likely to blur the distinctions between them and confuse family loyalty with business reality.

These considerations are magnified, in most instances, by the narrow vision of most business owners who believe that they and they alone have the requisite skills, savvy, guts, and knowledge to run the business. Many business owners will talk about turning over the reins to the younger generation, but they often do not follow through. In some cases, an owner will anoint a successor—a family member or outsider— and then emasculate that person either by constantly challenging his decisions or, worse, never giving him the authority to make decisions and assume responsibility for failure.

This book is not designed to offer psychological advice or insights to business owners about management succession. It is designed to help business owners understand that without an effective plan for management succession, the business owner will be left with only two options: he can sell his business (or take it public, which is almost the same thing), or he can let his heirs worry about it after he's gone. Both of these options are uncertain and unpredictable and they offer no comfort to the owner's family or to his employees that there is a plan to take the business forward.

When I meet with business owners to discuss management succession, I try to get them to focus on their real goals for the future of the business. I try to get them to see that it is possible to devise a structure or structures for management succession that will still allow an owner to have meaningful input and, yes, even *control* if he insists on that—but without hamstringing the potential for growth that is the lifeblood of any business. First, however, an owner has to accept the fact that the future of his baby, his beloved company, will depend on the skill, knowledge, and energy of others. Once an owner accepts that reality, the rest gets much easier.

It is not hard to understand why an owner feels this way to begin with. He either started the business, inherited it, or bought it a long time ago. He's poured his life, his entire being into that business and he's seen it grow and prosper under his leadership. He has been the linchpin, the decider of last resort, and he believes—sincerely believes—that without him, the chances for future growth and success are dimmed considerably. Après moi, le déluge!

Don't talk to him about young, fresh graduates armed with glossy MBAs. What actual business experience do they have? Don't try to get an owner to rely, suddenly, on his oldest child—or not so oldest child—who still won't clean up his room.

Thus, one key, critical element about management succession is that it is a *process*, an evolutionary process. No one expects to step into a leadership role, much less CEO role, at a company with no experience. But this can happen. Without getting too morbid about it, think about that hypothetical plane crash where the entire management team perishes. It happens. The result is not only catastrophic for their families and friends, but also for the business they have managed.

One of the primary goals of a management succession plan is the ability to train leaders, to provide seasoning, to give younger managers experience in the various aspects of the business. The key here is not only to provide that training and experience, but also to involve senior management in a mentoring program that will guide the younger managers on their paths to leadership. *Sink or swim* is not an ideal strategy for management succession.

This is true for a five-person management group or a fifty-person management group. In this case, size really does not matter. And it isn't necessarily easier with a smaller group. In a smaller group all of the egos, jealousies, competing goals, anxieties, and slights are magnified and in higher relief because there are so few people involved. So in some respects, it is harder to create a mentoring environment in a smaller group than in a larger one. But that does not diminish the need to do so.

One set of skills is to identify or hire talented people. Another set of skills is to provide these young, talented aspirants with an environment that cultivates their skills and hones their excellence. If it is true—and I believe it is—that a company's most important asset is its people, then it is also true that one of the most effective ways to use those people is to have them mentor younger managers and give them the benefit of the senior managers' hard-won experience and expertise.

In later chapters, we will explore the issues and complexities of both types of succession in more detail. We will also explore how both of these disparate sets of issues converge into a complete whole and a succession plan that offers a variety of solutions to both types of succession.

Before doing that, however, we need to delve into one of the most critical aspects of any succession plan: the issue of valuation. Simply put, before we can identify the best alternatives or options for an effective succession plan, we must be able to determine what the business is worth. This is critical not only for the obvious tax considerations that come into play, but also because an owner must have something other than his best guess as to what his business is truly worth. While it may seem more directly related to ownership succession and issues of transfer values, business valuation is also important for management succession because an owner will want a benchmark by which to measure and evaluate future performance and future success or failure.

Chapter 8

Valuations—Why They are So Important

> *Costello: You gonna be the coach, too?*
> *Abbott: Yes.*
> *Costello: Do you know the players names?*
> *Abbott: Well, I should.*
> *Costello: Well, then, who's on first?*
> *Abbott: Yes.*
> *Costello: I mean the fellow's name.*
> *Abbott: Who.*
> *Costello: The guy on first.*
> *Abbott: Who.*
> —Abbott and Costello, "Who's On First?"

In every situation I encounter when I meet with people to talk about succession, there is, at the very core, one incontrovertible and immutable "nucleus" and that is the question of *value*. Whether we talk about gifts or sales of equity, direct transfers, transfers into trusts, stock purchases or Employee Stock Ownership Plans (ESOPs), and whether we are talking about ownership succession or management succession, all of these strategies depend ultimately on the core question of value. Namely, what is the business—or, more to the point, what is the *equity* in that business worth?

The true answer to that question is that absent a willing buyer, no one really knows. The lack of certainty about valuation, however, does not diminish its importance or the necessity for obtaining an independent valuation for any succession plan. A good valuation is the bedrock principal that guides the formation, structure, and operation of any effective succession plan.

Notwithstanding this lack of certainty, there are some basic aspects of business valuations that are fairly straightforward. First, the basic rule is that a valuation should be based on the fair market value of the asset—in this case, the equity of a business. Fair market value can mean many things, believe it or not, but with regard to a privately owned business—where there is no trading market for the equity, no stock listed on the NYSE or NASDAQ, and no foreign markets such as the London Exchange—what constitutes fair market value can be more subjective than you might think.

The traditional definition of fair market value and the one used by the IRS and most valuation experts, is the price that a willing buyer would pay for an asset and a price at which a willing seller would sell that asset—assuming the buyer is under no compulsion to buy and the seller is under no compulsion to sell—and where both parties have reasonable knowledge of the material facts.

But getting past these "magic" words to a real understanding of value is a complex task. It's given mathematicians and business consultants the opportunity to create an entire industry over the methodologies and applications relating to valuations.

There are numerous methodologies one can use in valuing a business, but most of them can be reduced to three essential ones. The first is known as the income approach. A second method is known as the market approach, and finally, there is the asset approach.

The income approach bases value on the ability of the business to generate income or profits. This is done by examining projected cash flows over a specified period of time (typically five years) and then discounting those projected cash flows back to a present value using some range of cap rates or discount rates. This is usually referred to as a discounted cash flow analysis. Another way of using the income approach is to analyze a capitalized free cash flow using a specific rate of return. Got that? Don't worry if you haven't. In both of these methods, the future earnings capacity of the business forms the basis of valuation.

The market approach uses comparable publicly traded companies or recently purchased companies to compare what they are trading for—or the sale prices at which they were sold. Sometimes finding comparable companies can be challenging and it's usually not a very reliable method by itself. If there are numerous publicly-held companies in the same industry, then—after adjusting for differences in size, capital structure, market share, and other variables—this approach can give some sense, at least in a macro way, to what this business might be worth.

The asset approach simply subtracts the company's liabilities from its assets, resulting in a net worth or book value calculation. Sometimes with this approach, a multiple is then applied to reflect a premium for intangible values, or simply to estimate future growth.

Usually in a professionally determined valuation, the valuation expert will employ all three approaches and then decide which of them, either singly or in combination, the expert feels is most appropriate.

Whatever the methodology, the number crunching spits out an initial value. If one were considering a business valuation for purposes of seeking a sale of the business or even for a public offering, there would be further discussion of premiums or market value enhancements. One would look to multiples of earnings or cap rates to maximize the value of the business. The goal is, of course, to determine a present value based on some corollary to expected future performance. Also, to the extent there are "intangible" assets, such as patents or secret formulae, they might bump the value up as well.

However, when seeking a valuation for succession planning, the goal is not to maximize value, but rather to take that initial value and apply a variety of discounts to bring that value down. This is where the fun really begins, because invariably the valuation expert will apply certain discounts to reach a discounted fair market value. This can be used primarily for ownership succession planning, but also to set a realistic benchmark for management succession that may involve some form of equity transfer as well. It is also typical that a valuation for ownership succession purposes—where the owner plans to transfer equity to family members—may produce a different result than one intended to be used for stock options or some other form of equity designed to accompany a management succession strategy. Why? The owner will usually want to see a larger discount apply to equity that he proposes to transfer to family members than he would want to apply to his management team. Let it be said that independent valuations are just that—independent. In a perfect world the purpose of the valuation should not affect, much less dictate, how a valuation expert performs his task; however, in the real world, it is not uncommon for the owner to disclose to the valuation expert the purpose of the valuation and that information simply cannot be ignored.

Valuation discounts typically fall into two categories. One discount relates to the fact that the equity is not publicly traded and therefore has virtually no liquidity. This discount is usually referred to as the *lack of marketability discount*. It is an appropriate discount because a buyer of this asset will not be able to sell it or otherwise realize any increase in value without a more protracted and complicated sales process and also because there is no public market test for that increase in value.

A second discount applies where the equity to be transferred does not constitute a majority of the equity in the company; this discount is referred to as the *minority interest discount* or *lack of control discount*. Again, this is readily understandable, because any future buyer of the asset will recognize that his risk of ownership is higher because he won't have the ability to control the management or governance of the business, much less the ability to dispose of his asset when or if he decides to do so.

These discounts are used cumulatively to adjust the value of a marketable, controlling interest for the risk that owning something that the buyer is not readily able to liquidate. If the ownership does not include control—that is, if it is less than 50 percent of the voting power—there is also a risk of owning an asset over which the buyer cannot exert control. For one thing, the buyer might not be able to decide when or if the asset should be sold. These are not gimmicks or tricks. They are readily accepted by lawyers, accountants, financial advisors, and even by the IRS; however, tension does not usually arise over whether or not these discounts are appropriate, but rather over their magnitude.

Sometimes, aggressive valuations will deeply discount the basic fair market value calculation by as much as 65 percent, but in recent years the IRS has successfully challenged the more aggressive ones. When the discounts stay between 35-40 percent, there is usually—but not always—less of a controversy with the IRS. Unfortunately, there is no bright line or clear benchmark regarding what amount of discount is "safe." This is what the valuation expert really earns his fee for gauging. After all, if there is ever a contest or dispute over valuation, it will be the valuation expert who has to defend his discounts before the IRS or in court.

Why are these discounts so important? They are important because of the need to establish an acceptable base value for any gift scenario or a sale. The value of the gift or the sales price will be based upon this valuation. That value is more likely to be sustained or accepted if it comes from a truly independent party. It is no overstatement to claim that the entire success of the transaction will hinge upon the supportability and credibility of the valuation. So getting it right is critical. If you get too aggressive and lose to the IRS, then the taxable gain on your sale or the amount of gift tax you must pay on a gift, will rise, and sometimes spectacularly so. It can be so corrosive, that you may feel as if you have gotten no benefit from the transaction at all.

Getting a fair discount, a reasonable discount, is not only prudent and reasonable, but also it is an accepted and acknowledged facet of any valuation. Just don't be too greedy or aggressive. It's just not worth it.

This is why I cannot stress enough the need to get a reputable, recognized firm to provide the valuation. Valuations are not cheap, nor should they be, because they need to be thorough and complete. The valuation expert needs to take the time to learn about the business and its future plans. Since the valuation expert knows that in any dispute or controversy with the IRS, he will have to testify and support his reasoning and their conclusions. A well-reasoned, thorough valuation is the best insurance that an owner can obtain if he's going to embark on an ownership succession strategy.

Here is one final point about valuations. A valuation will "speak" as of a certain date. The equity or business will be valued as of a given date—usually the end of the most recent fiscal year of the company. It is important that the valuation be conducted as soon as possible after the valuation date. If the valuation isn't completed until a year after the valuation date, then its conclusions will be suspect for being obsolete. Again, there is no bright line or clear benchmark as to how long after the valuation date the valuation should be completed, but as a general proposition, I would say within six to nine months after the valuation date. If it is longer than that, then there can be significant questions about the reliability of the valuation, due to intervening circumstances. For example, if the business earned substantially more in the intervening period between the valuation date and the completion date, the discounted valuation might be more easily challenged or questioned.

Chapter 9

Ownership Succession—Giving it Away

Death is not the end. There remains the litigation over the estate.

—Ambrose Bierce

Now that I have described the general differences between ownership succession and management succession and we've tiptoed into the murky world of business valuations, let's get into more details about the various components of succession planning. I'll begin with ownership succession because it's the topic that most people think about when they think about succession planning.

At the outset, let's remember that there are really only two ways of transferring ownership. You can give it away or you can sell it. There really aren't any other alternatives, and despite all the complications and myriad variations one can dream up, the basic two alternatives remain.

Gifts

We'll begin by talking about gifts. This appears to be a pretty simple concept. I own something. I want to give it to you. I sign something that says I'm giving it to you and *voilá*, it's done. Isn't it? Maybe—or maybe not.

Let's examine this a bit more thoroughly. In order for it to be a true gift, two things must occur. First, the person making the gift, usually called the "donor," must intend to make that gift. That intent can be manifested by something in writing—a deed, a bill of sale (really a misnomer since it's a bill of gift, but no one ever uses that term)—or it can simply be a letter or other document that tells the world that the donor wants to give something to someone else. Or the donor can simply say, "I want to give you this stock." Of course, it's always better if the intent is expressed in writing, but it isn't absolutely essential. The really critical element is to be able to demonstrate the donor's intent to make the gift.

The second component, and the more problematic one, is that there must be delivery or completion of the gift by which the donor disposes of his ownership. Normally, this is straightforward, too. The owner signs a stock power that accompanies his stock certificate. That stock power and the stock certificate are handed to the recipient—the *donee*. Wham, bam, the gift is complete. In today's electronic age, with publicly traded securities, most of this is handled through intermediaries and stock transfer agents, but the concept is the same. The donor has fully and completely divested himself of any and all ownership of the stock. However, life is not always this simple.

To see how serious this matter of delivery can be, consider this real life story that has only recently become public. In 1993, Henry Bloch (of H&R Block fame) and his wife purchased a Degas painting known as *Danseuse Faisant des Pointes* ("Dancer Making Points") from a gallery in New York. The painting, not surprisingly, was of a beautiful ballerina. Unbeknownst to the Blochs and to the gallery from which they purchased the painting, it was a stolen painting. It had mysteriously disappeared from its true owner, the copper heiress Huguette Clark, in 1992 or 1993 and had been accepted by the gallery to sell shortly thereafter. The gallery was unaware of the fact that it had been stolen and sold it in good faith to Mr. and Mrs. Bloch. Ms. Clark, a renowned recluse who avoided all publicity and notoriety, never reported the painting as missing. When the true facts came to light in 2005, Ms.

Clark wanted the painting back, but Mr. and Mrs. Bloch wanted to keep it in their home where they had proudly hung it among their well-known collection of Impressionist art. The Blochs didn't want any publicity either, and neither side wanted to fight the matter out in court, so a settlement was reached. The Blochs agreed that the painting was in fact owned by Ms. Clark. In return, Ms. Clark agreed to donate the painting to Mr. and Mrs. Bloch's favorite museum in Kansas City and the museum agreed to loan the painting to Mr. and Mrs. Bloch for their lifetimes, after which it would return to the museum—together with the Bloch's other Impressionist art collection that they had previously agreed to donate to the museum. It sounds like a win-win-win for everyone, but now they had to complete this transaction. So, one day in Kansas City, an attorney for Ms. Clark appeared at the Bloch's home. The painting was removed from the wall and handed to the attorney (painting restored to rightful owner). The attorney dutifully walked out of the house with the painting to a car where a representative of the museum sat waiting. The attorney gave the painting to the museum representative (the gift). The museum representative then handed the painting back to the attorney (the loan), who delivered it back to the Blochs and it was replaced on the wall. To an outsider, nothing had happened, but legally, the painting had been restored to its true owner and had been donated to a museum, which then had loaned it to the Blochs. The ballerina had made a complete pirouette. Not bad for a painting that was worth many millions of dollars. That's how serious the matter of delivery is.

Gifts with Strings

What if the donor attaches some strings to his gift? Suppose he says to the donee, "Here's my stock, but I want to reserve the right to vote the stock for ten years, so sign this proxy." Or, what if the donor says, "Here's my stock, but I want the dividends for the next three years." Has the owner made a gift? Has he completed the gift? Suppose he gives the stock to a trust he established for his children and he's the trustee. Has he truly made a gift? Lawyers and IRS agents have field days with questions like these. We won't dwell on the legal technicalities, however. Just know that there can be complications with gifts, and if you want to make a real gift, be prepared to give up your ownership rights and claims.

We'll move forward and assume that the donor has intended to make a gift and has completed the gift. What else could go wrong?

Unintended Consequences

Imagine that the owner has given some stock to his child on the eve of that child's marriage. There's no pre-nuptial agreement because the two kids love each other—and to discuss, much less require, a pre-nuptial agreement would show that one kid doesn't fully trust the other. So, despite Dad's best efforts, there is no pre-nuptial agreement. With tears of joy in his eyes, Dad signs over stock to the child, delivers a stock certificate and stock power to his child or to her representative and the gift is complete. Three years later, the married child is disconsolate and the marriage is over. Divorce proceedings have commenced. What happens to the stock? Dad will be surprised to learn that his child's spouse may well own half of it. This may not be what he envisioned, much less desired.

Having thought of this problem and knowing that his child won't want to sign a pre-nuptial agreement, Dad puts the stock in trust for his child and (hopefully) his grandchildren. His best friend is the trustee, and when the unhappy news of divorce surfaces, Dad hopes to be able to terminate the trust if it's not irrevocable, or at least prevent the spouse from getting his hands on it. Depending on the terms of the trust, this may or may not work. What if the company is an S corporation, which (with few exceptions) requires that all shareholders be individuals, not entities? Certain types of trusts can qualify as an S corporation shareholder, but has the owner made sure that the trust is a qualifying trust for this purpose? Did he think about that at the time? What if he didn't?

If the trust mechanism works, what happens if the child remarries? Is any of that stock now in trust available for the children of the second marriage?

The complications don't have to involve a third party. Suppose the donor makes the gift, the child is gracious and appreciative, and the donor feels really good. Then, a few years later, the child has proven to be a big disappointment. He's become a spendthrift, dropped out of college or grad school, and has become too fond of an addictive substance. What happens now?

The basic answer is that nothing good happens, unless the owner has dealt with the complications in an agreement that covers these issues and more.

Shareholder Agreements

In a separate chapter, we will discuss the ins and outs of shareholder agreements (or their equivalents in partnerships or LLC operating agreements). For now, it is sufficient to note that among all the various documents and agreements that are used to document gift transactions or other dispositive transactions, no agreement is more important than this one. Agreements between the business owners, especially family-member transferees—regarding the governance of the business, limitations on transferability of their ownership interests and what happens to those interests upon death, disability, divorce, and other life altering events, (including those we mentioned above)—are critical; they provide predictability and avoids disputes. Even with regard to gifts of equity, the need and importance of such an agreement cannot be overstated. No agreement, no matter how carefully drafted and how thoroughly it is vetted, can cover every possible situation. Life is just too random and too crazy for that. So, one must be prepared for the unexpected and unanticipated and trust that most situations can be covered and the number of unanticipated ones will hopefully be very few. Moreover, just because no one can think of every possible contingency does not mean that he shouldn't deal with those that he can.

Family Limited Partnerships or LLCs

Another method for transferring ownership via gifts is through a vehicle known as a family limited partnership or family limited liability company. The business owner creates one of these entities, transferring his stock (or some portion of it) and he retains a small percentage (usually 1-2 percent) as a general partner or managing member to retain control. He then makes gifts of limited partnership interests or LLC interests to his children. Since the value of the limited partnership or LLC interests will be discounted for the discounts we discussed before for lack of marketability and for minority interests, these transferred interests generally won't result in any significant gift taxes. The owner has gotten most of his value out of his estate and has transferred ownership without giving up control. This strategy may also afford the owner an additional benefit in that his interest may be immune from attachment by creditors, although creditors may be able to take an assignment of the economic benefit of his interests. This all sounds pretty good and it can be an effective tool in the succession planning arsenal when used judiciously. The problems that usually arise relate to the size of the discounts—which we've already discussed. Also, the IRS is particularly wary of family limited partnerships and LLCs. The creation of these entities is often a "red flag" for the IRS and often produces audits or examinations of tax returns. The IRS tends to examine them very closely, especially regarding the discounts. Furthermore, the IRS may challenge the transaction entirely if the partnership or LLC does not have a valid business purpose. This could have serious tax consequences for the owner who may end up being taxed on his gifts and lose the entire benefit of the transaction.

One significant advantage of using the limited liability company structure as opposed to the limited partnership structure is that with an LLC, all members of the entity enjoy the benefit of limited liability for the obligations and liabilities of the entity. In a limited partnership, the general partner (the business owner) remains personally liable for the obligations and liabilities of the partnership and it is only the limited partners who reap the reward of limited liability. This can be mitigated if the business owner first creates a corporation that then becomes the general partner, but the issue of limited liability is an important one to consider. That's why the LLC model is being used more and more today, despite the fact that there is less law on the books or in the courts to confirm some of these issues, while there is a larger body of law that supports the limited liability and other aspects of a limited partnership.

Proper planning

The potential scenarios are as varied and complex as one can imagine. The bottom line is that one cannot predict or prepare for every contingency or unanticipated outcome. What one *can* do is know that these unhappy events do occur and often when you least expect them. So, the point is if you want to make gifts, plan for them and structure them with as many safeguards and protective rights as you can.

Taxes

I'm sure most readers know that with any gift there are gift tax consequences. Generally, one can give $10,000 worth of assets to each child, each year and, with his or her spouse, $20,000 per child per year, without any gift tax complications. Also, there is a lifetime gift exclusion of one million dollars. So, until you reach that level of giving, there is no gift tax. But, keep in mind that old specter of value. You may think that the stock you are giving away is only worth $10,000, but the IRS, if it chooses to challenge your gift, may claim a higher value; if it is successful, you could owe a gift tax. This is not to say that one should get an independent valuation for each gift or even at the start of a planned giving program, but one should keep the valuation issue in mind every time.

There is another significant aspect of gifts that I want to mention. When one makes a gift of property (stock, real estate, jewelry, etc.) the cost or basis of that property carries over to the donee. As an example, if I give my wife real property that I own and it's worth one million dollars, but I only paid $400,000 for it, then when I give it to my wife, she will have a "basis" in that property of $400,000, not one million dollars. So when she sells the property, her gain on that transaction will be the difference between her basis ($400,000) and the sales price. If, however, I sell that same property to her or she obtains it from my estate upon my death, then her basis is raised (lawyers and accountants use the term "stepped up") to her purchase price from me (if I sell it to her), or to its fair market value at my death. So, if she subsequently sells the property, her basis is now much greater and her taxable gain therefore much less. This is just one more reason to be very careful about gifts and to make sure that the donor fully understands the tax and other consequences of making those gifts.

Keep the Gift Arrow in the Quiver

Despite these complications, a properly constructed gift program can be a significant and effective part of a succession plan. It helps remove some of the equity from the owner's estate, creates good will, and promotes family harmony; well, it can promote family harmony— although I am mindful of the old Chinese proverb, *No good deed goes unpunished.* Whether an owner chooses to make outright gifts to his children or make gifts to various types of trusts, he can effectively spread ownership across his family landscape and provide some means of economic reward even if those family members have nothing to do with the business. The main point of this discussion is that a gift program is only a piece (and in most instances a small piece) of any effective succession plan.

Charitable Gifts

I am not going to discuss the topic of charitable giving. That's an entirely separate subject beyond the scope of this book. Normally, charitable giving of stock involves gifts of publicly traded securities and not stock in privately owned companies. Also, charitable giving, even of privately owned stock, can sometimes be part of an estate plan where some type of charitable remainder trust or similar vehicle may be appropriate. But even in those instances, the *corpus* or asset that is used is a readily marketable asset—not stock in the owner's business. I will leave the subject of charitable gifts of privately owned securities to the estate planners and their ilk. If you have an interest in that type of gift, please talk to them.

Chapter 10

Ownership Succession—Selling It

I feel the same way about managing that I do about investing: it's not necessary to do extraordinary things to get extraordinary results.
—Warren Buffett

Just as the concept of giving equity away seems simple at first, so does the concept of selling equity. At first blush, it doesn't seem like rocket science. I own something. I have a price in mind now that I want. I've found a buyer willing to pay that price, so we enter into an agreement and I sell equity to that buyer for that price. I deliver a stock certificate or other evidence of ownership and the buyer pays me the purchase price. No big deal.

As anyone who has ever tried this knows, however, it isn't as simple as that. Selling and buying equity is not the same thing as selling or buying a car, a refrigerator, or a television set. At least not where there is any established trading market. Why? Because one of the primary reasons that one sells or buys equity, versus a car, a refrigerator, or a television set, is that the seller believes the equity's value is as good as it's going to get—keeping in mind the seller's reasons for selling. The buyer, however, believes that the value of that equity is going to increase and he wants to make sure he can sell it at some point in the future if that increased value materializes. So, with equity, as opposed to most other assets, there are both short-term and longer-term goals and expectations.

Also, while the seller may be motivated to sell for lots of reasons—some of which we will soon explore—with equity, as opposed to other types of assets, the seller wants to make sure that he keeps control and that if something bad happens to the buyer, the seller can reclaim the equity he has sold.

In the context of succession planning, an owner may desire to sell equity for a variety of reasons. First, he may wish to use a sale as part of his estate planning, and we'll delve into that topic shortly. Second, he may wish to bring in a minority partner whom he thinks, if all goes well, may become his successor and will want to buy the rest of the company. Third, an owner may want to "take some chips off the table" and liquidate some of his built-up value by selling equity to a private equity group or some other value-oriented strategic partner. Fourth, an owner may want to provide equity to his key employees, and since his company is not publicly held, the concept of stock options may not be a meaningful alternative. Selling equity to them, as opposed to giving stock to them or providing them with stock options, may be a better solution. Finally, if the owner wants to consider using an ESOP, a sale is the preferred strategy. Let's take a closer look at each of these alternatives.

Estate Planning

The basic notion is simple. If an owner sells equity while he's still alive, then that asset is no longer part of his estate. The proceeds of that sale may be part of his estate, but that is now a liquid asset, as opposed to the illiquid asset he previously owned. Thus, the owner's estate avoids the problem of quarreling with the IRS (or with his heirs) over the value of that equity. Plus, if any estate tax is due, the estate has the liquidity with which to pay that tax. This avoids the specter of having to sell the company in order to pay the owner's estate tax liability. Years ago, Coors Brewery went public primarily in order to satisfy the estate tax liability of its founder, Adolph Coors.

But typically, an owner will not want to sell all of his equity during his lifetime. That's tantamount to a sale of the company and while that may be an alternative, it really isn't part of succession planning. If an owner sells all of his equity during his lifetime, then he has taken succession planning off the table because there's nothing to succeed to. So, for our purposes, we won't deal with a complete sale of an owner's equity. We will focus on partial sales and, typically, sales of minority interests—because as important as it may be for an owner to liquidate a portion of his equity—maintaining control over the business is an equal if not higher priority. As we will see, there is a constant tension between the owner's desire to provide equity to family members, a minority partner, or key employees, on the one hand—and his ardent desire to maintain control.

If the sale of a minority interest is an outright sale to a third party, then the structure and tax consequences are pretty straightforward. The third party owns the equity and the seller has capital gain—presumably long-term capital gain—on the difference between his basis or cost, and the sales price. The buyer's basis in the equity is his cost.

The remainder of the equity still owned by the owner remains in his estate, however, and may be subject to valuation issues upon his death.

Of course, the owner could simply cause the company to issue new equity to the transferees. While that may keep the control issue at bay, it does nothing to alleviate the owner of any of his equity and hence nothing to diminish the size of his estate.

Sale Alternatives

The circumstances of how the owner structures a sale of his equity will depend in large part on the intended purchaser. Keeping in mind the ever present issue of valuation discussed in Chapter 7, an owner may want to structure a sale to family members very differently from how he structures a sale to a third party, or sales to key employees.

There is also a third tension-engendering component to any of these sales, and that has to do with how the purchaser will *pay* for the equity. Presumably, family members and key employees will not have the financial strength or liquidity to pay in cash for the equity at the time of purchase. With regard to sales to third parties, it is of course desirable to have the purchase price paid in full at the closing, but depending upon the amount, that may not be feasible either.

A variety of techniques exist to overcome the payment problem, but most of them involve the purchaser giving a promissory note to the owner for all or a portion of the purchase price; the equity is then pledged back to the owner as security for this debt. This is invariably the case with a third-party purchaser, but with family members or key employees, one strategy is to pay bonuses or other incentive compensation to the purchasers, which they can then use to amortize the purchase debt. Keep in mind, however, that this additional compensation is also taxable to the family employee or key employee, so the amount of additional compensation that is paid is usually higher—so it can also cover, in whole or in part, the income tax consequences of the additional compensation. What this means for the owner is that his payroll is going to increase, sometimes substantially, in order to fund this purchase program.

With family members who are not employees, the purchase note can be paid from dividends on the equity or, if the owner is truly generous, the debt can be forgiven over time. Be careful, however, because usually when someone forgives a debt owed by someone else, that creates taxable income for the debtor—under the theory that he has received taxable income equal to the amount of debt forgiven. So, in most cases, it is far better to make sure that the purchase note is actually paid.

You might be thinking: *What happens if the true value of the equity, taking into account appropriate discounts, is, say, $100 per share, but the owner wants to sell the equity to his children or to key employees at a lower price? What are the consequences of doing that?* Generally, if there is an established value for the asset and the owner sells it for less, it can be considered a *bargain purchase,* in which event, there can be adverse income tax consequences to the purchaser because he will be treated as having received more than he actually paid. And normally, that additional amount will be treated as ordinary income, not capital gain. In most privately owned businesses, the question of determining whether there has been a bargain purchase is difficult to establish, especially where valuation discounts are appropriate. Even though it may be hard to establish whether there has been a bargain purchase, the parties should nevertheless be careful in dealing with this issue because if the IRS challenges the transaction, through tax audit or otherwise, it can get very expensive to resolve this. All the more reason for using proper valuation techniques from the outset.

Estate "Freezes"

One strategy often employed that helps an owner dispose of some of his equity and create ownership possibilities for his family is using a technique commonly known as an *estate freeze.* This gets complicated to explain, but as I promised, I will try to keep it simple.

Essentially, an owner makes a sale of a significant portion, but less than 50 percent of the equity in his company, based upon the discounted value determined through the independent valuation process we've described. He does this by first creating a single-member LLC that we will call "Newco," of which he is the sole member. This is very important for tax purposes if the company is an S corporation, because the single-member LLC will be "disregarded" for tax purposes and the S election will not be lost. The owner contributes the equity he is going to sell to that LLC in exchange for 100 percent of the LLC interests. The owner then creates a trust for his family and he sells LLC interests (not the actual stock in the business corporation) equal in value to the percentage of ownership in the company held by the LLC. The purchase price for those LLC interests is paid via a promissory note from the trust to the owner. The interests in the LLC purchased by the trust are now no longer part of the owner's estate. The asset that is in his estate is the balance due on the note. Thus, the value of that portion of his estate formerly represented by the stock now held in the LLC is "frozen" at the level of the note. Any future appreciation in that stock will be realized by the trust.

This transaction does not remove the interests in the LLC from the owner's estate that he retains which has a value equal to the value of his retained percentage interest in the LLC. Thus, if the owner sells 45 percent of his LLC interests to the new trust, that value is now removed from his estate, but he still owns 55 percent of the LLC interests, equivalent to 55 percent of the value of the stock held in the LLC. Thus, any future appreciation in that stock will be part of his estate. Of course, he can make other transfers of other LLC interests, by gifts to this family or to charity, or he can sell those LLC interests as well. Again, the reason he may not want to do that is that it will result in relinquishing control over the business and most owners prefer to retain that control—even if it means they don't remove the entire value of their stock from their estates.

Chapter 11

Assessing Family Members and Management

*During my eighty-seven years I have witnessed a whole
succession of technological evolutions. But none of
them has done away with the need for character in the
individual or the ability to think.*
—Bernard Baruch

We now diverge from dealing with almost "pure" ownership succession issues to a discussion of ownership succession in the context of sales to third parties and employees. In this context, the owner must deal with ownership issues as well as management succession. It is obvious that in most cases, any discussion of management succession will undoubtedly involve a discussion of equity transfers. For the most part, however, those transfers will involve minority equity interests, at best, and the owner does not lose control of the company.

Before dealing with the various types of equity transfers involved in management succession situations, it would be helpful to focus attention on what the goals and objectives of management succession are and how they impact decisions on ownership.

When an owner begins to think about management succession, he inevitably conjures up an entire web of issues to untangle in order to get a clearer picture of what is really at stake and what is really going on. So, let's discuss the issues in discrete segments. First, we'll discuss management succession in the context of family members, then in the context of minority partners, and finally, in regard to existing and future management.

Management Succession in General

Libraries and bookstores (and now e-book catalogs) are filled with all sorts of business management treatises that deal with management succession. A simple online search lists plenty of articles about the subject.

More to the point, any business owner knows in his gut the same things that all the experts say. First, identify the position. Then, evaluate the people. Then, create opportunities and hold people accountable. Then, be ready to follow through. To some extent, therefore, discussing management succession may seem like so much hot air. However, there are important factors an owner should consider when he thinks about management succession.

First, this process is not scientific; nor is it overly complex. The human element and the complexities of human relationships are what make the process difficult. In most privately owned companies, the senior management team is pretty small. Usually, it's four to six people. Those people know each other very well, not only because they spend most of their time together, but also because they have learned to depend on one another. Trying to pick and choose among them in a succession process is not only hard; it's painful. Someone is going to be disappointed, no matter what. On the one hand, that's part of the management evolutionary tree and it can lead to disaffection and departures. On the other hand, the process presents an opportunity for the owner to assess the leadership skills and strategic thinking of his management team. Most of the time, these qualities are not evaluated because of the day-to-day pressure of the business world.

All of this is compounded if family members are part of the management team. The non-family management group may think that management succession is a foregone conclusion—surely the favored kid or sibling will take over. That may not be so if the owner isn't confident in his family's ability to run the business. In fact, he may well decide that the bifurcation of ownership and management that we've been discussing is exactly the structure he needs—keeping ownership—or at least controlling ownership—in the family, but turning management over to trusted and more capable people.

Second, by going through the process of checking his management team for what I will refer to as leadership skills, an owner will often find that there are gaps in his management team that he needs to fill. I'll give just one example. More and more companies today are learning that they need an executive to manage the glut of information that streams into and out of a company over the Internet, through social media, e-mails, and other forms of electronic communication. To deal with the problem of information overload and information overflow, more and more companies are creating the position of Knowledge Information Officer or Chief Information Officer. To the extent that an owner sees a real need for this type of person, he may or may not find that one of his existing management team members can handle the job. One way to make that determination is through an analysis of the strengths of the management team that goes beyond their individual performance.

A third benefit, if you will—running counter to the possibility of departures of key personnel—is the possibility of enhancing the management team's cohesion by involving it in the evaluation process so that its members feel more connected with the company and more invested in its future. Not everyone is cut out to be a CEO and most management people know, or at least understand, that they may not be CEO material. This does not diminish their value or importance to the company. Through a proper management evaluation process, this can be identified, with the result that rather than leaving if one is not chosen to be CEO, a trusted and valuable key employee may feel more secure and more valuable where he is because his talents and skills are appreciated.

What I am really saying is that the process of management succession entails a much more strategic and long-range view of the company; that broader vision is not only healthy—it is essential for any business that plans to grow and prosper.

Let's take a look at some of the issues an owner confronts when he starts to consider management succession. First, we'll look at family matters.

Family

How does an owner designate or select which, if any, of his children or other family members (nephews, step-children, spouses of children, as examples) will be his successor as the primary manager of the company? If his family members are grown and out of college or graduate school, they may have already self-selected. Some may have already chosen other careers. Some may have indicated that they have no desire to come into the business. Others may feel that even if they have the desire to become involved with the company, the owner is too controlling; the friction and conflicts that might arise from working closely with him will not be worth the effort or the risk that the chosen one or chosen few will ever actually grab the brass ring.

The owner may feel that none of his family members is ready to take over the reins, but that with seasoning and mentoring, they could. Or, he may feel that none of his family will ever be capable of managing the business. In addition, the owner might decide that one of his older children is in fact well-suited to the task and is ready to be the anointed one. The last thing the owner wants is to create disharmony among his family. Yet, how can he avoid doing so when such an important decision is looming?

An owner faced with this predicament has several choices. He can make a decision and announce it to the family without any previous discussions, input, or analysis. He can put several family members in various management roles and see what happens. He can hire a management consulting firm to help select which family members are best suited for particular roles within the company. None of these alternatives sounds very appealing. Is there a better route through this thicket? Yes, there is.

The keys to effective management succession planning as it relates to family succession are two-fold. First, the owner must be straightforward and honest with his family. He's got to tell them what he is thinking: what criteria he is looking for in a successor and whether he feels that any (or some, or all) of his family members can qualify. It should not degenerate into a contest between children or siblings, where corrosive competition—not to mention envy or jealously—is almost bound to arise. It's far better to confront the issues in an honest and forthright way. Get the family together and discuss the subject. The owner needs to tell his family how he really feels and what he believes is best for the company and for them. The family needs to understand that the owner is going to make decisions; he's going to take into account those factors and talents that he believes are best exemplified in the person or persons he wants to take over the business. In most cases, I find that whether or not the family is happy with the owner's decision, they are very happy that he has made a decision and announced it. The uncertainty and tension that exists when the issue of management succession is on everyone's radar screen—but no decision has been made—can be excruciating. It is debilitating to the family and to the business. It's far better and ultimately *calmer* for the owner to make up his mind and communicate his decisions to his family.

If the owner feels that no one in the family has the requisite skills or abilities, then he should announce that he is going to look outside the family for management succession. He should also tell the family that, in this case, some amount of ownership will undoubtedly be sold, given, or awarded to "outside" management, be it current employees or a new business partner, or both—but that voting control will remain within the family, at least for the foreseeable future. Or, he may announce that as part of his management succession plan, control over ownership may also pass outside the family. Whatever the case and whatever the owner decides should be communicated directly and with candor.

The other factor an owner should always keep in mind regarding management succession is that he needs to trust his judgment, his instincts, and his experience. No one knows the business better than he does and no one knows his family better (most of the time). I'm often asked whether an owner should seek input from family members as he goes through his analysis for management succession. In general, I discourage this. This cannot be a decision made by committee. Almost invariably, if an owner seeks input from his family, he's going to alienate more people than he would by simply announcing his decision. This is not to say that an owner can't discuss the subject of management succession with his family, but it should be done with the unequivocal message that the owner will make his decisions based on his own mindset and values.

In trying to reach a fair decision about management succession, an owner will need to balance the talents and skills of family members with those of existing management. Indeed, the very process of thinking about management succession may create opportunities to fill in gaps in the management team that appear more clearly, perhaps more starkly, when the owner looks through the lens of succession.

Existing Management

It goes without saying that the best way for an owner to assess the succession capabilities of his management group is to make sure a solid evaluation system for management is in place. Oftentimes, management evaluation is an informal, ad hoc process that may involve nothing more elaborate than the owner taking his management team to lunch and praising them for their hard work. And when year-end approaches and bonuses are awarded, there may or may not be any corresponding evaluation of management's successes and challenges over the past year. This is a serious mistake for lots of reasons, including retention, morale, profitability and more, but it is equally as serious a mistake when the owner has to decide about management succession. What is he going to base his decisions upon? It isn't the same as with family. The owner can think very subjectively about his family and in the last analysis, no one can question him. Not so with non-family management. These are the people on whom the future of the company will depend. If they do not feel they have been fairly treated, they will leave. If they do not feel they are being given a fair opportunity to perform and to be rewarded for their performance, they will leave. Not only will they leave, but also they will leave loudly, meaning they will become public critics of the company they have just left. None of those consequences is good for the owner, or for the company.

It's very important, therefore, for the owner to implement a solid, comprehensive evaluation program for his management. It should be formalized and regularly monitored to make sure it is effective.

A key element of any good evaluation program is the self-evaluation component. Many companies do not use this at all—or if they do, it's a very subjective part of the process. Often, it's just a narrative written by the employee describing his performance and his own view of his strengths and weaknesses. It's far better to have a written form for the employee to complete; it can be created with great care and can provide valuable insights into the employee's sense of his own accomplishments and challenges. Often an employee's self-evaluation will cast a more critical eye on himself than any third-party evaluation would ever show.

An evaluation program, no matter how rigorous or thorough, is not going to provide a roadmap for management succession—not unless it includes an analysis of leadership skills, integrity, common sense, and one of the most important criterion, a balanced personality. Can the employee roll with the punches? Is he too sanctimonious or self-serving? Can he laugh at himself and with others? Evaluation systems don't usually include these factors and, to some extent, they are not as critical in considering typical management performance. They are very critical for succession issues, however. So—in addition to the more traditional evaluation metrics and questionnaires—as an owner begins to think about management succession, he needs to ask a whole new set of questions and get a much broader sense of his management team's capabilities.

There's a big difference between performing well at a designated level and performing well at an entirely different level. There are stresses, pressures, and conflicting points of view that a CEO must deal with that are unique to that position—and it's not a position everyone is qualified to fill. Evaluations are only one small piece of the management puzzle.

In addition to a rigorous evaluation program, an owner must also consider an effective incentive program to reward management's performance and to serve as part of the compensation benefits to attract talented management. We will talk about various types of incentive programs in a later chapter. For now, it is sufficient to note that when an owner starts to think about management succession using his existing management, he must make sure he has established a strong, stable incentive program that not only rewards performance, but also that provides powerful incentives for his people to stick around for the long term.

Let's assume that an effective evaluation program is in place and that appropriate incentive compensation plans are working. What does the owner do next? How does he navigate the Chutes and Ladders ™ of management succession? Isn't it just as subjective as thinking about his family?

To some extent, any decision about management succession has subjective elements. This is art, not science. As any owner of any thriving business knows, many of his business decisions are "gut" decisions, based on his experiences, his knowledge of his industry and company, and his sense of which decisions just feel right. Management succession is no different in that respect.

With management succession, however, there are some objective criteria an owner can employ. First, he has his evaluation program to rely on, hopefully augmented by the more succession-oriented factors described above. In addition to the evaluations, the owner can rely on his interactions and experience with his management team. He's bound to know their strengths and weaknesses. He can rely on that experience to help guide him along the path to succession.

In some cases, an owner may want to bring in an outside management consulting firm to help him assess the capabilities for leadership among his management team.

Whatever the case, the owner will be much better served if he has established some criteria of his own. He should identify those factors and characteristics that he feels are most important in selecting a successor. And in thinking about those factors, an owner must look ahead and try to identify those characteristics that will be needed for the next ten to twenty years—not just the tried and true ones that may seem eternal. The owner should be prepared to look for talents and skills that he may lack or that are very different from those skills he brought when he became the owner. For example, in today's business climate, dealing with social media is a vital component of any business's success. Social media probably didn't exist at the time the owner came along, except in the form of cocktail parties and trade shows.

During this process, the owner may discover that despite his best efforts to hire and keep talented personnel, no one really is qualified to assume the mantle of CEO. In that case, the owner has two options.

First, he can work with his existing management team to try to develop the leadership and management skills he feels are necessary in any successor. This will require the owner to meet with his management team and discuss these qualities with them. He needs to let them know that he's considering succession and that his team must rise to a new level and begin to develop these skills. If they cannot assure him that they are capable of meeting these goals, he may have to look outside the present team.

Sometimes, owners bring in new talent or try to fill gaps in the team's capabilities with new people—without letting the existing management group know in advance. In my opinion, that's a very bad idea. There's nothing wrong with bringing in fresh talent, especially where gaps in the group's skills are known, but to do so without informing the management group will seed discord and disharmony among the group and may well impede—if not prevent—any new personnel from gaining the support and cooperation of the old team.

Whatever process an owner chooses, he must follow through with it expeditiously. There's nothing worse than a long, drawn out succession contest. It not only is bad for morale, but also it will directly impact performance and, ultimately, the bottom line. So, the trick, if there is one, is to make the decision as quickly as possible and move on. It shouldn't be too precipitous, however, because then no one will trust the result. Finally, once the owner has made a decision and announced it, he must follow through and give his support—not only to his designated successor, but also to the rest of the management team.

The biggest reason that management succession fails is that the owner will commit one of two equally unpardonable sins. First, he decides that he doesn't like anybody. He still thinks he's the best boss and so he just abandons the project. It's much worse than letting air out of a balloon. It's much worse than deciding to abandon the new distribution center in Las Vegas after two years of hard work. Why? Because by initiating the process, the owner has signaled two very important things. First, he's going to make a decision about the future and how the company will be managed. There will be certainty about succession, and the questions and rumors will stop. Second, the owner is going to set a path for that future and enable fresh thinking (not that his is outdated) to have an impact. There's a sense of renewal and energy that permeates the company. Abandoning the process, however, kills all those notions. It stifles incentive and it makes the owner look indecisive and uncertain.

The second sin is that the owner goes through with the process and even announces a decision about succession—but then he has second thoughts. After all, he is the owner, right? He can do that, right? So, he does. He says, "I made a mistake. I'm not ready for this and neither is my successor. We'll think about it, as Scarlett O'Hara once said, tomorrow."

For the same reasons that the first sin was so bad, so is the second. Maybe it's even worse, because the hopes and aspirations—not only of the successor but also of the other key players—were raised and then dashed on the rocks. It's not easy coming back from this kind of false start. In fact, it often leads to the very last thing an owner may want at this particular time in his life and in his company's existence—a sale of the company because the management team has become dysfunctional.

Chapter 12

Sales of Equity to
Third Parties and Employees

*However beautiful the strategy, you should occasionally
look at the results.*
—Sir Winston Churchill

The most obvious example of a sale to a third party is when an owner decides to bring in a partner whom he may be grooming to be his successor and he needs to sweeten the deal with equity. In privately-owned businesses, this is a very traditional method of acquiring top talent, because any highly qualified potential partner will be savvy enough to want a piece of the action. He knows that his future wealth will come from ownership, not from compensation.

These transactions can be structured in many different ways. However, the common elements are the following: (a) the equity will usually come from the company, but it can be provided by the owner; (b) the price to be paid will be privately negotiated between the parties without the use of an independent valuation; (c) there will be a vesting schedule; (d) provisions will be added relating to clawing back the equity upon certain events (death, disability, retirement, resignation, or termination); (e) there will be provisions relating to restrictions on the transferability of the equity; (f) there will be provisions on governance— whether the new employee will be an officer, a director, or when and how that status can be achieved; and (g) there will be provisions that will require the employee to sell his stock if the owner sells his equity (usually called *tag along*), and if the owner decides to sell his equity, he must include the equity of the employee (*drag along*). There may or may not be provisions relating to the new employee's right to purchase the owner's remaining equity, but this can get very complicated and is usually addressed later on after the owner and minority partner have established a good, trusting relationship. All of these provisions can be found in the original purchase documents, or in a separate shareholders' agreement. (There it is again.)

In some cases, rather than selling equity directly to the new partner, the owner may offer options to purchase equity. This allows the owner to retain full ownership and control until and unless the option is exercised. Depending on how many conditions the owner wants to set before the option can be exercised, it may keep the partner from actually owning any equity for some time.

Further, the payment problem has to be addressed. Typically, the new partner won't be able to pay for the equity at the outset. How he is allowed to make payments and get the equity is a subject of direct negotiation, but the owner recognizes this financial limitation and usually this works out. Either the partner signs a promissory note, as discussed above, or he pays for a certain percentage of the equity each year from bonuses or other incentive compensation he may receive.

Sales to Employees

When we discuss the subject of transferring or selling equity to employees, we are of course primarily talking about another aspect of ownership succession. However, providing equity to key employees—or in some instances, to all employees—is both a subject of ownership succession and management succession. After all, an owner who wants to designate a successor, be it a single person or some group of people, will want to make sure that those same people have an economic incentive to assure future growth and profitability. To do that, the successor will need to have "skin in the game," and the purpose of this discussion is to describe how that happens.

With privately owned companies, one of the most effective incentives is to sell stock to key employees. There are a number of ways to accomplish this. One of the most often used ways is for the company to adopt a restricted stock or membership interest purchase plan. This can be a very important incentive in hiring and retaining talented people, and we will review the basics of these plans a little bit later. For our purposes, though, as noted earlier, this type of plan does not help the owner divest himself of any of his equity because the sold equity comes from the company as newly issued equity.

There is no reason, however, that an owner could not establish a restricted plan for key employees, using his own equity as the currency for that plan. In this way, the owner sets aside a certain amount of his equity to be sold to key employees based on whatever criteria he may select. Usually, a committee of key employees is formed to manage the plan and to determine which employees are eligible to participate and how much equity they can purchase. Normally, in plans that involve new equity from the company, the cap on the total amount of equity that can be sold through the plan is generally around 10-15 percent of the total equity in the company. With owner-generated plans, it can be whatever amount the owner decides.

There is an important reason that an owner may want to consider a company-sponsored, restricted stock plan—and here is where the interests of the owner in thinking about ownership succession merges with his interest in management succession. Even though a restricted stock plan won't help with ownership succession per se, it has a lot to do with hiring and keeping talented, qualified employees who will form the basis of the management team in the future. A restricted stock purchase plan can be a very powerful tool in attracting high quality people to work for an enterprise and to provide them with meaningful incentives to earn a share of the pie.

Criteria for participation in a restricted plan can be as varied as the owner desires. Participation can be based on the following: length of service; performance metrics (achieving certain net income goals or productivity goals, for example); cost savings; or any other objective criteria that an owner can imagine. It is always better to have objective criteria, because without them, employees who are excluded or who can only purchase very small amounts are apt to regard the plan with suspicion and the incentive element will be lost.

We have already talked a bit about shareholder agreements, and here again is another reason they are important. If the owner is going to open up the equity door and let more people in, then he must have some method of determining what happens to the equity upon certain events. Many of these contingencies (death, disability, retirement, resignation, or termination) can be covered in the plan document itself, but if the equity has fully vested (a topic we will discuss shortly), the plan restrictions may not apply and it's always better to have them contained in a binding shareholders' agreement.

I just mentioned vesting. Let's discuss that now. Many of you may be familiar with this term if you have studied or even held stock options of one kind or another. It is often the case—almost universally the case—that stock options "vest" over some period of time. This means that the holder of the option only gets the right to exercise portions of the option that vest over time. For example, an option may vest 20 percent per year and therefore not fully vest for five years. Therefore, the option holder can only exercise 20 percent of the option each year. But vesting can apply in many circumstances beyond the option context.

I'm sure most of you are familiar with vesting schedules in retirement plans or 401(k) plans, where an employee's account does not fully vest for some period of time.

Well, vesting can also be a significant component of equity plans. In restricted stock plans, the purchaser may only get control of a certain percentage of the equity over a specified period of time. If the employee dies, retires, resigns, or is fired before his equity is fully vested, then the unvested portion is forfeited and he usually is required to sell the vested portion back to the company or to the owner (in the case of an owner-structured plan) at the original purchase price or at some other pre-determined value.

Vesting serves two primary purposes. First, it provides a meaningful incentive for the employee to stick around and to continue to be productive. Otherwise, he won't get to keep his equity. Second, it delays the eventual dilution of ownership so that the owner can see how well his participating employees are doing. If they are succeeding, then all is fine in the kingdom. But if some are not, then they can be terminated and the unvested equity is lost.

Even though stock options are not normally found in privately owned businesses, there is no reason they cannot be used. The main reason they are not used is that since the equity has no established trading value or capability, the option holder is not able to sell some of the stock or equity he receives upon exercise in order to cover the tax liability he may face when he exercises his option. I will explain some of the intricacies of stock options in a later chapter.

Before leaving this subject, I need to discuss one other significant tax concern involved in sales of equity, and this has to do with something called the "Section 83 problem."

Section 83 of the Internal Revenue Code provides certain rules for recognizing taxable income (or not) when equity is sold or given to employees in exchange for services. In most cases—due to vesting issues or requirements that an employee forfeit his equity if certain events occur (he resigns, for example within a certain period of time)— these contingencies are known in the tax jargon as "substantial risks of forfeiture." If property such as stock is awarded to an employee for services—or even if it is sold to the employee at a fixed price, but still is subject to one of these substantial risks of forfeiture—then Section 83 provides that the employee does not recognize any income for compensation paid to him at the time the equity is given or sold to him, and that taxable amount is deferred until the risk of forfeiture lapses. Technically, the value of the equity is not measured until the restrictions go away. So, even if the employee paid fair market value at the time of sale, that's not necessarily going to be the value that measures what he actually receives when the restrictions lapse. The following example shows how this can produce some very tough results. Suppose that an employee buys stock for $10 per share in 2012 and that is the stock's fair market value at that time. However, the terms of the plan provide that if the employee leaves within five years, all the equity is forfeited to the company (or to the owner in an owner plan) and the employee gets his original purchase price back. I've kept this example simple and have avoided the option of partial vesting over the five years, which is the more typical case. Five years go by and the employee is overjoyed, because now his equity is fully vested and no longer subject to forfeiture. Now, however, the stock is worth $30 per share. What happens? Well, the employee is deemed to have received compensation equal to the difference between what he paid for the stock ($10 per share) and what it is worth at the end of five years ($30 per share). This means a $20 per share amount of ordinary income in the fifth year. That could be a sizable bite. Is there a way to avoid this result? The answer is *yes*.

Section 83 permits the employee to "elect" to declare income in the year he gets the equity, even though he may lose that equity in the future. If the amount he pays is equal to fair market value, there is no taxable income to him. If the stock were just awarded to him for services, then, per the example above, he would be deemed to receive taxable, ordinary income of $10 per share. In addition, any future appreciation the employee may realize—upon sale of the company for example—would be taxed as capital gains, not ordinary income. While this is a better result than waiting for five years and having a huge tax bite, it does have certain disadvantages. First, the employee is declaring receipt of income when he may *lose* the equity in the future. He will never get a credit for the taxes that he pays in year one if he forfeits his equity down the road. Second, if the stock does not appreciate, but rather goes down, then he has paid taxes for nothing.

These disadvantages notwithstanding, it is usually better for the employee to make the Section 83 election at the time he gets the equity, because the amount of taxable income he then realizes is going to be small—compared with what he may be required to recognize down the road when the equity has substantially appreciated. After all, if he's going to bet on the company to grow at least partially through his own efforts, then he should be willing to "bet" on that outcome at the start.

Elements of a Restricted Stock Purchase Plan

There are six key elements to any restricted stock purchase plan: aggregate number of shares or interests that can be purchased; eligibility criteria; determination of purchase price; method of payment; vesting and clawbacks; and restrictions on transferability. Many of these same elements exist with respect to other types of equity-based plans and are also involved with direct sales to third parties as mentioned before, but I will spend more time discussing them here. Again, this is not designed as a legal treatise on these topics, but I feel that before anyone can intelligently decide whether or not to create one of these plans, he should understand the ins and outs of them.

Aggregate Number of Shares or Interests

In establishing one of these plans, the first thing an owner must decide is: *How much of his equity is he willing to transfer to employees via this plan?* Remember, this plan is only one strategy in an arsenal of strategies an owner can use to provide equity-based incentives for his employees. So, this doesn't have to be the only vehicle. Further, the use of this type of plan is designed more to provide incentives for employees than it is to provide estate minimization for the owner. This is especially so if the plan is a company plan, where the company will issue new equity to employees, as opposed to a plan utilized by the owner to dispose of some of his equity.

Whether the plan involves owner's equity or new equity from the company, the end result is the same. The owner's original equity position will be diluted by the amount of stock or interests that employees acquire through the plan.

In practical terms, the aggregate amount of equity that an owner will devote to one of these plans typically hovers around 15-20 percent of total equity. In some cases, it is much less. It is rarely more than this. The principal reason is that the owner wants to make sure he retains voting control, and with other elements—such as stock options or a possible sale of equity to a new investor or business partner—an owner will want to make sure that the aggregate amount of equity that he makes available to all possible purchasers is less than 50 percent.

Eligibility Criteria

The most basic criterion for participation in one of these plans is longevity. An owner should be reluctant to allow a brand new employee access to real equity for several reasons, not the least of which is that the owner does not know whether a callow employee will turn into a star or a dud. Also, a new employee will have little sense of the culture of the organization or a demonstrated commitment to help build the company. Then, too, since the aggregate amount of equity that can be purchased is limited, an owner will rightfully want to reserve that equity for people who have demonstrated the key qualities he expects of his employees: intelligence, loyalty, dedication, collaboration, common sense—the list goes on and on.

However, just as being too fresh is a concern, so is an eligibility requirement that is too long. If an owner demands too much longevity before an employee is eligible to purchase equity, the incentive can be lost because no one wants to wait too long; too many things can happen, including termination, death, or disability.

The owner must search for a balance in establishing this criterion; typically, the eligibility factor is one to two years.

So, the first criteria are usually set as a benchmark—in order to be able to purchase stock in the plan, an employee must have been continuously employed for a certain period of time.

The owner doesn't have to worry too much about initial eligibility, because these plans also typically include a vesting requirement or a reverse vesting requirement. We will discuss those matters shortly.

Another criterion would be some type of performance metrics—either an individual set of metrics for each employee, or an aggregate set of metrics for the company. Examples of individual metrics are: increased productivity in the employee's department or area of responsibility; number of new customers (for sales people); operating efficiencies or cost savings (manufacturing people); or expense reductions or savings (administrative people). Company metrics could include revenue growth of a certain percentage or amount or growth in net income.

Purchase Price

In these types of plans, independent valuations are usually not obtained. The owner sets the purchase price based on a financial benchmark—usually book value or a multiple of book value. The purchase price could also be tied to net income, or any other financial standard the owner may select. The object here is to set a price that is non-dilutive—or the least dilutive—to other equity owners; however, is not necessarily a price that a third party would pay to acquire a significant equity stake in the company. Normally, the kinds of discounts we discussed before—relating to gifts or other estate planning techniques—will not apply in these circumstances, primarily because the purposes of these plans are entirely different.

The purchase price will also vary from year to year as future economic results produce new or different values. If profits go up, for example, then the purchase price for that year will go up.

Payment

Since most employees who participate in these plans do not have the financial liquidity or resources to pay for their equity at the time of purchase, the plans include various methods of payment options. The basic method is for the employee to sign a promissory note for the purchase price, with a modest interest rate and a fairly extended maturity date. Payments can be made annually, usually from bonuses or other incentive compensation paid to the employees. If there is a liquidity event, such as a sale of the company or a public offering, the note will mature at the closing of that event when the employee will presumably receive cash for his equity.

Other methods of payment include payments tied to incentive compensation but without a promissory note—or simply a deferred payment schedule, such as minimum payments for some period of years with a balloon payment at maturity.

The main point is that the owner should not place undue burdens on his employees to pay for their equity. The requirement that they pay for their equity must be balanced with a fair and reasonable opportunity for the employees to do so.

Vesting and Clawbacks

A vesting component would mean that an employee could purchase a certain amount of equity each year that he is continuously employed for up to five years, for example. Once he purchases the equity, he owns it and has the right to vote that equity (assuming it is has voting rights) and he is entitled to any dividends or distributions.

A reverse vesting requirement would mean that the employee can purchase a certain amount of equity at the outset—but if he leaves or is terminated, or dies or becomes disabled—the company has the right to purchase the equity for its original purchase price. This is sometimes referred to as a clawback.

Clawbacks can also apply to equity that is fully vested for the same events or occurrences. This allows an owner to be sure that he can recover the equity should an employee leave or die so that the equity does not become owned by strangers.

Transferability

Normally, the equity purchased through a restricted stock purchase plan cannot be transferred by the employee to anyone. Not only are there securities law implications for transfers, but also the owner will not want the employee to dispose of his equity so that it ends up in the hands of someone who may not be an employee. Also, if the purpose of allowing an employee to purchase equity is to give him an incentive to work harder and produce more, allowing him to dispose of that equity defeats that purpose.

For the same reason, these plans do not typically provide for transfers to family members as part of the employee's estate planning. With larger investors or equity holders, this is permitted in some cases, but not usually with equity issued in connection with these types of plans.

So, an employee who acquires stock through a restricted stock purchase plan and has held that equity beyond any required vesting period—and who has fully paid for that equity because his note has been paid in full—must expect to hold that equity until there is a liquidity event.

Other restrictions on the equity or opportunities to dispose of that equity would typically be contained in a shareholders' agreement. We have referred to this type of agreement many times in this book and I have devoted an entire chapter to this subject. It's really important.

Options

Most companies that offer options to their employees are publicly owned and have an active trading market in their stock. This is because if an employee exercises an option, he has a readily available trading market—so he can turn around and sell the stock if he needs to pay any taxes resulting from the exercise of the option, or just to convert the equity into cash for other needs. Nevertheless, options can be a valuable device for hiring and retaining key employees in privately owned companies that have a longer-term strategy that includes a possible public offering, so we will spend a fair amount of time discussing them.

Without being too simplistic, but just to make sure we all know what we are talking about, an option is a contractual right to purchase something in the future at a fixed or otherwise currently determinable price. If the holder of the option decides to exercise it, the company or other person who holds the asset that is subject to the option has no choice but to sell the asset at the option's exercise price.

There are two types of options when it comes to equity in a company. One is known as an "ISO" or incentive stock option, and the other is known as an "NQSO" or non-qualified stock option. The term *qualified* refers to the tax code. And there are significant tax differences between the two types. Incentive stock options are issued pursuant to written stock option plans that meet certain requirements of the tax code. Generally, to "qualify" as an ISO, the option must have duration of not more than ten years and the exercise price of the option must be equal to the fair market value of the stock on the date the option is granted. This is another reason that these types of options do not find their way into the equity programs of most privately owned companies. Determining fair market value without an active trading market can be difficult. Normally, a company will not want to engage in an independent valuation each year to set a truly independent test for fair market value. However, working with the company's accountants and financial advisors, it is still possible to come up with a meaningful valuation. There is also a limit on the maximum number of shares an option can cover.

ISOs are only available to corporations and only cover stock. They are not available for membership interests in LLCs or partnerships.

The advantage of an ISO is that when the option is exercised—even if there is a significant difference between the exercise price and the then-current value of the stock—there is no tax to the employee at that time. Also, if and when the employee sells the stock he obtained through exercising the option, the gain he realizes will be capital gain. There is no ordinary income component with ISOs and Section 83 (discussed above) does not apply.

NQSOs are very different. There are no rules about exercise price or duration, and there are no limits on the number of shares or amount of equity that can be covered with such an option. Since they are not "qualified", NQSOs can be issued with respect to any type of equity, stock, LLC interests, or partnership interests.

As you would expect, the tax consequences of exercising an NQSO are also very different than with ISOs. First, when an NQSO is exercised, there can be ordinary income to the person exercising the option, because the difference between the exercise price and the then-current value of the equity covered by the option will be treated as ordinary income to the employee. Earlier we discussed the ability of a purchaser of equity being subject to forfeitures to make an election under Section 83, to peg the amount of ordinary income at the date of purchase. However, the holder of an option cannot make a Section 83 election when he gets the option. He hasn't acquired anything at that time, so there is no basis on which the election can be made. Consequently, the measurement of value doesn't begin until the option is exercised and the employee is deemed to have received compensation equal to that difference when he exercises the option.

So, even if the stock covered by the option remains subject to substantial risks of forfeiture—for example, the employee may have to sell the stock back at its original cost if he leaves the company within a certain period of time—he cannot make a Section 83 election until he exercises the option.

There's one other big difference between these two types of options. With ISOs, a company does not get a tax deduction for compensation paid to employees when an ISO is exercised, or if and when the employee sells the stock. With NQSOs, the company *does* get a deduction at the time of exercise—if there is a difference between the exercise price and current fair market value—because the employee will be treated as having received compensation equal to that amount, unless the stock remains subject to restrictions that bring Section 83 into play.

Why would an owner want to consider using options in a privately owned business? There are several reasons. First, the owner does not give up any equity at the time an option is granted. Exercise will depend upon future performance; if the company does well and profits increase, then the owner should be happy to share that wealth by allowing employees to participate through options. If there is no future growth or enhanced performance, the value of the equity in the company is not likely to increase and the options won't be exercised because there is no value to them.

Another reason an owner may choose to issue options is that an employee doesn't have to pay for anything at the time the option is granted. It's a no-cost benefit at the outset. If the option has value later on because the equity value has exceeded the exercise price, then the employee will want to exercise the option. He may be able to fund that purchase through his own financial resources, with a bank loan or through some other form of extrinsic financing that does not require the company to provide funding capabilities—as is the case with restricted stock purchase plans.

Finally, just as issuing an option defers the company's commitment to issue more equity, so does holding an option defer a decision about acquiring that equity. This gives both the company and the employee time to evaluate the merits, not only of acquiring equity, but also of continuing with the company as an employee. While it is true that an employee holding an option does not have "skin in the game" to the same extent as an employee who has purchased equity directly, an option holder has just as much reason to want to see the company grow and prosper; yet he doesn't have to worry as much about how he's going to pay off that note he would have signed had he purchased equity directly.

Employee Stock Purchase Plans (ESOP's)

I am now going to write a bit about another form of succession planning that is often brought up as an effective and tax-motivated strategy for passing ownership down from the founding owner to his employees. This strategy involves using a device—a trust actually—in what is commonly called an Employee Stock Ownership Plan or Employee Stock Ownership Trust. The acronym for this device is an ESOP or ESOT.

This strategy came along in 1974 as an incentive for owners to transfer stock in their companies to their employees. The carrot—and it's a big one—is that if the owner uses an ESOP and adheres to certain rules, then the money he receives for selling his stock can be sheltered from federal and state income tax for as long as he lives. That's a very big deal.

How does an ESOP work? Essentially, setting up an ESOP involves the following steps. First—no surprise—the owner obtains an independent valuation of his company. With ESOPs, as opposed to other types of transactions where valuations are so critical, the desired outcome is not necessarily the lowest possible value. Indeed, from the owner's perspective, the opposite is usually the case.

The next step is for the owner to decide how much of his stock he wants to sell. The owner then sells that stock to the ESOP and takes back a promissory note for the purchase price, which gets paid over time. Where does the ESOP get the money to pay for the stock? Typically, an ESOP will borrow the money from a bank and use the proceeds to pay the owner. How does the ESOP repay this debt?

Herein lies one of the main issues with ESOPs. The only source of revenue for an ESOP is contributions from the company, which—as long as the ESOP owns at least 30 percent of the outstanding stock—are tax deductible to the company, or through dividends from the company that are paid with respect to the stock owned by the ESOP. These contributions or dividends can only be paid out of the company's earnings, and it must be able to pay those dividends and still have enough capital to run the business. Thus, the amount of stock an owner sells to an ESOP is a function not only of how much stock he wants to sell, but also of how much stock the ESOP can afford to buy. An owner can structure sales over a period of years, and there is no requirement that a sale be "all or nothing." However, for most companies, there needs to be a large enough group of employees to justify setting up an ESOP. It is possible for the ESOP to obtain a bank loan to pay for the stock it has acquired, but in today's environment, that becomes a less likely funding option. It is something that should be considered, however,

With ESOPs, there are also issues to be dealt with regarding what happens when an employee leaves or retires. As with most other plans, an ESOP can have a vesting schedule, but once the shares are vested and an employee leaves, he is usually entitled to keep his share of the stock that the ESOP purchased or he can sell those shares back to the ESOP for cash.

Since ESOP's are considered a type of "qualified" employee benefit plan, they are subject to the rules and requirements of The Employee Retirement Income Security Act of 1974, also known as ERISA. ERISA imposes a number of requirements and restrictions on qualified benefit plans, so if an ESOP is something you may want to consider, you should definitely consult with an advisor who is very knowledgeable about these types of plans.

It is beyond the scope of this book to discuss ESOPs in greater detail. For the right company, with the right make-up of employees and an owner motivated to transfer a significant portion of his ownership to them, ESOPs can be a solution—and a part of an effective succession plan. There are drawbacks—as with most plans—and so, again, careful planning and forethought are very important in considering whether to use an ESOP.

Chapter 13

Shareholder Agreements

*You never have trouble if you are
prepared for it.*
—Theodore Roosevelt

Of all the advice in this book, I personally think there is no more important subject than the subject of this chapter—shareholder agreements. When I talk about shareholder agreements, I include not only the separate agreement that is entered into by shareholders of a privately-owned corporation, but also the comparable provisions that one typically finds in operating agreements for limited liability companies and in partnership agreements. So, while I may refer for ease of reference to the term *shareholder agreement*, understand that I'm talking about the same issues that one faces in an LLC or a partnership.

Why is this subject so darn important? For the simple reason that without one, there is chaos, confusion, dissension, disagreement, litigation, calamity, hail, fire and brimstone! Yes, we'll have trouble in River City! I say "trouble," to quote that esteemed philosopher—Professor Harold Hill.

It's a sure fact that if an owner doesn't include such an agreement in his business, much less in his succession plan, then all his plans and schemes will be for naught. Once an owner decides to share his ownership with others, be they family members, management, or third-party investors, it is imperative that he put in place a set of rules and policies that govern the new relationships between himself and his fellow shareholders and, equally importantly, among the shareholders themselves.

Shareholder agreements may not provide certainty for all contingencies; no agreement can. A well-crafted shareholder agreement, however, can avoid most of the more common problems that confront multiple owners of a business.

When one breaks it down, there's really nothing too complicated about shareholder agreements. The issues with which such an agreement grapples fall into three well-defined areas. First, there are issues that deal with governance and decision-making. The second set of issues deals with transferability of the equity. The third set of issues deals with what happens to the equity upon the occurrence of life-altering events, including death, disability, divorce, retirement, termination of employment, or incompetency. As with any agreement, the alternatives are as varied as the personalities of the equity owners and there is no "form" that works for all situations. If we highlight the major issues in each of these categories, however, I think we can shed some valuable light on how to demystify and simplify the range of issues that need to be resolved.

Governance and Decision Making

In most cases, the original owner is not going to give up control of the company. He will almost invariably retain at least 51 percent of the ownership so that he can make most, if not all, decisions and many shareholder agreements say simply that. Any decision affecting the company—from hiring employees, to borrowing money, to selling the company—only requires a simple majority vote and the owner has that vote. End of story. Well not quite, or not completely quite. In most states, the law imposes certain fiduciary duties on the majority owner to take care of the minority owners. For example, if an owner decides to sell the company, but decides to issue to himself a second class of stock that would result in his receiving twice as much as the rest of the owners—such a scheme would probably fail if tested in court. He can't overreach. For the most part, however, he can continue to make the decisions without regard to the desires or wishes of the minority owners.

In other cases, the majority owner reserves the right to make most of the decisions. He may acquiesce, however, to allow a larger percentage vote—some call it a supermajority vote—to approve certain major events, such as a merger or a sale of the company. It could be two-thirds or 75 percent. The number doesn't matter as much as the fact that someone else besides the majority owner has the right to approve these major decisions.

A related issue is who gets to sit on the board of directors of the company. Ownership in and of itself does not assure anyone of a board seat. Usually, it does not. However, in a family-owned or privately owned business, the majority owner may wish to permit others to have board seats and really help him govern the business. Again, typically, the majority owner will keep control of the number of board seats, but it is becoming more and more common for minority owners to have at least one board seat. In situations where a third-party investor comes in, he will typically get a board seat and his vote will typically be required for any major decision.

In the last analysis, the majority owner will need to balance his desire to retain control with the important consideration that he needs to give his equity owners a voice in the governance of the company.

Transferability of Equity

This won't take long to discuss. The short answer is that there is no transferability in most cases. Minority owners won't be able to sell, pledge, or give their stock away. Period. That's the general rule.

In some cases, there can be exceptions for estate planning purposes. A minority owner may be allowed to transfer equity into trusts established for his family members or directly to family members. In these instances, the trusts and the other transferees must agree to become parties to the shareholder agreement and their equity will remain subject to the shareholder agreement. This preserves the sanctity of the agreement and assures all of the equity owners—not just the majority owner—that the equity will remain in friendly hands, or at least not be owned by strangers.

Shareholder agreements also typically include other transferability rules. For example, if a shareholder decides he wants to sell his equity, he may be required to offer it first to the company and then to his fellow shareholders. If they don't buy it, however, then it remains subject to the restrictions on the agreement and cannot be sold. What if a minority owner gets an offer to purchase his equity? In such a case the agreement usually provides that he must give the company and his fellow shareholders a "right of first refusal" to purchase those shares at the same price and on the same terms as he was offered by that third party. If no one matches the offer, then he usually can sell to the third party, but that third party must agree to be bound by the shareholder agreement. Again, this preserves the links to ownership. While it is possible in such a situation for the equity to become owned by a "stranger," it isn't likely, because it is highly unusual for a true stranger to be willing to purchase a minority interest where his influence is so small in a company where he has no other relationships.

In some cases where there are only two shareholders, the game can get even dicier. Some shareholder agreements include what some call a "shotgun buy sell" provision or a "put and call" buy sell provision. This type of provision allows one owner to set a price and to offer to buy his fellow owner's share at that price. However, the other owner can turn around and offer to buy the original owner's share at that same price; the original owner has to accept that counteroffer. The theory behind this type of provision is that it keeps one owner from setting too low a price, because if his offer is too low, his fellow owner can turn right around and buy him out at that same price. It sounds fair. It sounds reasonable. But it rarely works—and by "work" I mean without resort to litigation. Why doesn't it work? Well, these provisions don't take into account the financial condition of the parties at the time the original offer is made. For example, if owner A, who's flush with cash and doing well, knows that owner B is in financial straits and is having trouble paying his bills, owner A could make a low-ball offer, knowing that owner B could never match it. Owner A could therefore snatch away Owner B's equity at a very low price and there's little that owner B can do. I've seen these provisions in a number of shareholder agreements and they always make me cringe because I've seen how they can work. Sometimes it isn't very pretty.

Buy Sell Rights

In shareholder agreements, the corollary stream of issues that arises when one deals with restrictions on transferability is the set of issues that deal with the disposition of equity when a shareholder wants to sell, receives an unsolicited offer to purchase his equity, or suffers a life altering event. This is where proper planning and forethought are really vital.

In every situation involving the grant, sale, or purchase of equity, the recipient or purchaser is always looking to the future and trying to craft some type of exit strategy. The company or the majority owner needs assurance that in any of these circumstances, it at least has the right, if not the obligation, to get the equity back so that it doesn't fall into unfriendly or strange hands.

There are many different techniques and strategies to accomplish both goals. The most common ones are rights of first refusal, options to repurchase, and mandatory repurchase rights.

Rights of First Refusal

A right of first refusal is similar to an option. However, it's an option in favor of the company and the *other* shareholders. It basically works like this. When a shareholder receives an offer to purchase his equity, he must first offer that equity to the company or to his fellow shareholders, or both—with the same terms and conditions of the first offer. For a limited time, the company and then the remaining shareholders have the first right or option to purchase the equity on those same terms. Only if they do *not* elect to purchase the equity on those same terms, can the shareholder then sell the equity to the original purchaser and then only on the same terms contained in the original offer. One of the conditions to completing the sale with the original purchaser is that the purchaser has to become a party to the shareholder agreement so that the equity and the new shareholder become bound by the terms and limitations in the agreement.

Other Rights and Obligations to Purchase

The two other primary categories of events that give rise to purchase rights or purchase obligations occur when a shareholder leaves his employment, if he is an employee—either voluntarily or involuntarily—or when he dies, becomes disabled, becomes legally incompetent, gets divorced, or retires. In each of these cases, the company wants to provide a mechanism for the purchase of that shareholder's equity.

There is first the question of whether the company has the obligation to purchase the equity or just has the right to purchase it. Often, the nature of the triggering event will dictate the answer to this question. For example, upon death, the agreement may typically provide that the company will purchase the deceased shareholder's equity. In that case, the company will often purchase life insurance on the lives of its shareholders, to provide a funding source for the repurchase obligation. Or, the shareholders may form a trust or partnership that will purchase insurance on the lives of the shareholders, the proceeds of which are used to fund the purchase of the deceased shareholder's equity.

In most other instances, the company reserves the right to purchase the equity but is under no obligation to do so.

In cases where the owner retains a large block of the equity, a shareholder agreement can provide that the restrictions and limitations apply only to minority shareholders and not to the majority shareholder. While this may seem a bit overbearing, it is a reasonable exclusion in order to give the majority owner freedom of action in dealing with his company.

The critical question in all of these circumstances is: What will the purchase price be? It can vary a great deal, again depending upon the triggering event. For example, take the situation where an employee-shareholder is terminated for cause. He embezzled money, or he was insubordinate, or he had an improper relationship with another employee. In these circumstances, the company typically has the right to purchase that shareholder's equity for no more than what he originally paid; in some cases, the agreement can apply a discount to the original purchase price, due to the shareholder's conduct. In other cases, the purchase price can be pegged to book value or some multiple of book value, or to a multiple of earnings over some period of time that will take into account aberrant swings in profits.

Finally, in many cases, the agreement will provide that the purchase price can be paid in installments over some reasonable period of time, typically three to five years, with interest.

These same factors and issues arise whether or not the new shareholders are employees.

The company will want third party investors, even if they aren't shareholders, to be bound by the same restrictions on transferability; it will usually provide for some form of exit strategy because the investor will want some contractual ability to sell or dispose of his investment.

Sometimes the investor will demand a "put," meaning that at the end of some specified period of time, he can require the company to purchase his equity at a fixed price. Depending on the circumstances, this can impose a significant financial burden on the company. Proper planning is essential to make sure that the company will have the financial strength to purchase the investor's equity without adversely affecting the company's ability to continue to grow.

Although I've given just a brief summary of the major issues that an owner needs to confront in dealing with shareholder agreements, the reader can already see how important and necessary they are to prevent future disputes over how the company is managed and how its equity is treated.

One last point about shareholder agreements. For obvious reasons, it is better to create a shareholder agreement before the owner decides to bring in new investors or sell stock to his employees. This is especially true with employees, because they will be less likely to raise issues if they know that—as a condition to getting their equity—they must sign the shareholder agreement. Even with third party investors, having the agreement in advance is still a good idea because it will narrow the issues that will have to be negotiated. An owner should not make the mistake of believing that he can always deal with these issues later and that it's more important to get the equity distributed first. Just the opposite is the case. An owner can avoid much grief and tribulation if he just takes the extra time to think through these issues and have a well-crafted shareholder agreement ready to go at the time he announces his stock purchase plan or stock award plan.

Chapter 14

Stock Awards; Deferred Compensation

Snowflakes are one of nature's most fragile things,
but just look what they can do when they stick together.
—Vesta M. Kelly

If you have read the chapters that deal with how to dispose of equity to employees, you may have concluded that there must be a better way to provide meaningful incentives for your people—not only those whom you've already hired and want to retain, but also those whom you are looking to hire in the future. Let's face it; giving employees equity, selling employees equity, or granting them options to acquire equity can be complicated. It can be messy. You've got to worry about how to get the equity back if they leave, or if they have a life-altering event. You've got to worry about paying dividends to them. You've got to worry about "creeping dilution." By this last concern, I mean the perennial problem any owner faces when he thinks about disposing of his equity. There's only a finite amount of it (we won't address here the issuance of more equity to the owner—suffice it to say that gets very complicated, too), and if he disposes of too much to his employees, then he has to worry about how much equity he wants to transfer to his family. This is because in the back of his mind—and maybe in the front of his mind—there is the never-ending issue of keeping control of the company in his hands. So, how much is too much? How much is not enough?

Keeping in mind that an owner wants to do something to build a platform for succession, is there another way to get there without actually transferring real equity?

The answer is *yes*; there are a number of other ways to create some of the same benefits of owning equity without actually owning it.

I'll describe the most traditional methods, but as with some of the other strategies I've outlined in this book, I want to keep things simple. The basic, simple premise of all these other strategies is that there is always a trade-off.

If an owner transfers true equity, giving the new owner the right to vote and the right to receive dividends and distributions upon a sale of the company, the new owner gets real power. Even if the number of shares is small and relatively insignificant, it is real equity and carries real and substantial benefits—benefits the employee can see, touch, and feel. If and when that equity is liquidated—through a sale of the company, a public offering or some other means—the employee will realize capital gains if the equity has appreciated, which is the whole idea of transferring it to him in the first place.

With the quasi-equity strategies I'm going to describe, the majority owner gets the benefit of keeping all the voting control and distribution rights under his thumb. The employees, on the other hand, get only an economic benefit. They don't get to vote and they don't have a say in management. Their only right is to receive funds when and if certain events occur in the future, such as a sale of the company. Furthermore, the economic benefit they get produces ordinary income to them at a certain point, not capital gains.

Why is this so? Primarily because all of these strategies involve a form of deferred compensation. The reward does not materialize until some time in the future. There is no transfer of real equity, so the "asset" that the employee receives is not a capital asset but rather a form of compensation that is deferred until the occurrence of certain specific events. Therefore, the tax law will not allow employees to treat any gain on this asset as a capital gain. To the contrary, any gain will be treated as additional compensation and taxed at ordinary income rates.

As we describe these other methods, then, keep in mind the trade-offs they entail.

The most basic forms of deferred compensation are: stock appreciation rights; so-called "phantom" stock awards; and performance awards.

No matter what they are called, the essence of these arrangements or plans is that the company decides on an annual basis, usually, to award or grant certain rights to employees that have the same economic benefit as owning actual stock, but which defer the realization of that economic benefit until some point in the future. That point can be any of the following: retirement; a sale of the company; a public offering; or some other type of liquidity event, such as a merger with another company. As with option plans, these rights can vest over time, but the general premise is that the economic benefit, or award, is tied to an increase in value of the underlying equity from a benchmark value determined from the time the award is made to the time the liquidity event or retirement occurs. It doesn't have to be a liquidity event, however; it can be the passage of a certain number of years, or any other measurement the owner desires. The realization date is usually tied to a liquidity event because that is when the company will have the funds with which to pay the amount of the award.

This is important because for these plans to work from a tax perspective, the company cannot create a protected fund or reserve to cover its liability under these plans. It is possible to set up a certain type of trust, commonly called a "rabbi trust" or "secular trust"— where money can be held to fund these deferred plans, but the money must remain subject to the rights of creditors of the company. If the funds are protected from creditors or otherwise insulated, then the plan may be challenged by the IRS; the money could be deemed income to the employees when the awards are made, rather than later when the rewards are earned.

Generally, stock appreciation rights or phantom stock awards will measure the increase in value from a fixed value at the time of grant, typically book value, with book value at the future liquidity date. The measurement can be increases in profits, or any other metric the owner decides he wants to use. The differences among SARs (stock appreciation rights), phantom stock, and performance awards, are not great. Many people use the terms interchangeably. In some cases, SARs are deemed to relate to a specific number of shares, while phantom stock and performance awards are described as "units." In some cases, holders of phantom stock may be entitled to dividends and distributions, while holders of SARs typically do not participate in dividends or distributions. However, the common thread among all of these plans is the use of future growth (revenue, profits, book value, as examples) to reward performance.

If the employee leaves before the triggering date, dies before that date, or suffers another life-altering event before that date, the award simply goes away. It does not pass down to the employee's heirs or family. If he leaves or is terminated, the award is typically forfeited.

Chapter 15

Bringing it all Together

Nothing recedes like success.
—Walter Winchell

I hope it is apparent by now that for a business owner to create an effective succession plan, he must engage in a lot of planning and forethought. The array of components he needs to consider is quite large and varied, for he must weigh the needs and skills of his family with the needs and skills of his management. Then he must balance all of that with the needs and opportunities for his company to grow. Melding all of this into an effective succession plan can be challenging, but it can also be very gratifying. It is well worth the effort.

It should also be apparent that an effective succession plan is like a skyscraper. It has many parts that may seem very disparate—from gift programs to family members to deferred compensation plans for employees. I've tried to show that these discrete elements are actually complementary. Together they form, in the best cases, a system that works with the rest of the business aspects of the company in a smoothly functioning, multi-faceted business environment.

This is important not only for the family and employees, but also for the other stakeholders of the business—its customers, vendors, and related businesses that may depend upon this business for their own livelihood. While these other stakeholders may not voice their ideas or concerns about succession planning, any owner of a business can bet that the subject comes up whenever these other businesses start to think about the longevity of the owner's company or the future business plans for their own businesses.

Seeing how these various components converge in a holistic way is not that complicated. If an owner has analyzed his family situation and management team, he can propose both an ownership succession plan and a management succession plan that work together. If he has implemented an effective incentive system of compensation and rewards, he has provided the structural elements needed to forge a forward-thinking, growth-oriented business strategy; this can offer his family and his key employees a rewarding future and, equally as important, the opportunity for a harmonious relationship, whether the owner is still around or not. This is the essence of the business legacy that any owner wants to leave.

We have canvassed the landscape of succession planning with larger overviews of many aspects of them, and we have also drilled into some of those components in great detail. Having done that, we can now identify those factors or components that will herald the most effective types of succession plan.

For one thing, we know that an owner should begin the process before he, his family, or the business reaches a critical stage. This should be before a life-altering event occurs and before a potential shift in business ownership—via a sale or other liquidity event.

For another thing, we know that an effective succession plan deals with the two primary threads of succession: ownership and management. Not only does an effective succession plan deal with these two separate themes, but also it does so in a way that blends the owner's desires and goals for each thread into a compatible and coherent plan.

On the ownership side, we know that an effective succession plan provides for an orderly transition of ownership from the current owner to his family, to his employees, or both, or to a third party, with the possible combination of all three potential new owners. Also, in the best succession plans, this ownership change occurs over time; there is not a sudden or abrupt transition. In addition, or as part of this transition, an effective succession plan will provide for true equity or quasi-equity (deferred compensation) to be provided to key employees in a way that not only rewards them, but also provides substantial incentives for them to remain with the company—even if ownership control shifts from the current owner. At the same time, control over the business for the immediate and near term, if not longer, remains in the hands of the current owner.

On the management side, an effective succession plan includes leadership development and expanded management opportunities so that current management can spread their wings. If new or additional management is needed in a given area, then the succession plan is a useful tool in not only identifying those needs but also providing economic and ownership incentives to attract talented people to fill those needs.

We also have seen that effective succession plans create opportunities for the current owner to delegate more responsibilities to his key management and provide ways for his management to experience the challenge of strategic decision-making.

Effective succession plans also evolve. They are not static. To the contrary, their strength lies in their flexibility and adaptability to changing circumstances and unanticipated business conditions.

Therefore, a prototypical succession plan will include at least the following concepts and strategies:

First, there will be a mechanism for transferring ownership from the current owner. This may involve estate planning, gifts, sales to third parties, sales to family members, or sales to employees.

Second, all equity holders will enter into a shareholder agreement that will govern their management rights, their transferability limitations, and their dispositive rights.

Third, the owner will initiate incentive plans for his key management team. This can include direct sales of equity, stock options, or deferred compensation arrangements that may involve phantom stock or stock appreciation rights.

Fourth, the owner will embark on a leadership development or training program that will allow current management to stretch their skills and learn more about managing a company as opposed to a single division or department.

Fifth, the plan will create opportunities for evaluation and modification, depending on future events and circumstances.

Sixth, the owner announces the succession plan to his family and to his management, if not also to select customers and vendors.

With all of this in place, the owner can feel confident that he has accomplished a truly enviable feat and has done a great service for his family, his company, his employees, his customers, and all others who depend upon the vibrancy, stability, and forward-thinking attitude of his business.

Chapter 16

We Now Return
to Our Six Scenarios

*Inspiration could be called inhaling the memory of an
act never experienced.*

—Ned Rorem

Let's now go back and revisit the six scenarios I sketched in the first chapter to see how those scenarios might play out if a succession plan were in place at those times.

Scenario One (John meets with Albert):

John tells Albert that he's welcoming him into the family, and wants to explain to Albert how John has provided for the continuity of ownership and management of his company. Whatever Rebecca will own or inherit is now part of a comprehensive plan, and while John hopes that Albert and Rebecca have a long and wonderful life together, he has provided for security for his daughter and the rest of his family through a series of agreements that restrict and control what happens to the equity in the company. Furthermore, if Albert is going to become a key employee of the company, he needs to know that a management succession plan is in place and that John will be happy to describe the elements of that plan for Albert. Thus, whether or not John wants Albert and Rebecca to sign a pre-nuptial agreement, John has taken care to make sure that the equity in his company is protected.

Scenario Two (John and Rebecca):

John tells his daughter that he wishes her well in her chosen career—whatever that may be—and he does not begrudge her traveling for a while. The good news is that she doesn't have to worry about John or the company, because John has created a succession plan that will, among other things, provide security and economic rewards for Rebecca, even if she never works for the company. John may impose some strings on those economic rewards, but he doesn't have to worry about Rebecca frittering away her inheritance during his lifetime, and he has made provisions in his estate plan and in the succession plan that protect the company and the equity in the company for the future.

Scenarios Three and Four (John talks with his senior management; GEM's employees are talking among themselves):

Rather than wondering what is on John's mind, the employees have been told about the succession plan; they know where things stand and what the future may hold. They know that they will have a place in the company—provided they continue to perform—and there will be either real equity or substantial amounts of deferred compensation for them if that future performance comes about. There is no more uncertainty about John's plans. Moreover, they now know that a management succession plan is in place. Whether or not that plan has identified a specific successor to John as the CEO, GEM's employees know that there is a plan in place to assure the future stability and growth of the company.

Scenario Five (John meets with his family):

This can be the same scenario as the one in which John meets with Rebecca. Here, the family counsel contains more people, but the result is the same. The family knows what John has planned to do and that he has implemented a strategy to make that happen. Some may chafe under that knowledge, while others may see it as a great opportunity to become real leaders in the company, with strong mentoring from John. There's really no way to tell, but the fact that there is now some predictability for the future—and the fact that John has been proactive in creating the opportunities for that future success—should be applauded by everyone.

Scenario Six (the unsolicited offer):

I like this one the best. John can get as excited about this offer as he wants because he knows that whatever happens—whether the offer materializes into a sale of the company or not—he has established a clear path for sharing the economic benefits of that transaction, should it happen. He has also provided a mechanism, through the management reward or incentive plan he has implemented, for his employees to share in that benefit as well. Moreover, the buyer will more than likely be very excited and happy to learn that John's key management will stay. If the buyer doesn't want that, he has the ability to start fresh and replace them.

Chapter 17

Where Do I Go From Here?

When planning for a year, plant corn
When planning for a decade, plant trees
When planning for a lifetime, train and educate people.
—Chinese Proverb

The first step on your journey to an effective succession plan is to recognize that you can't start the process too early. Whether it takes you six days or six weeks to put a plan together, you should know by now that you have to begin while the subject is on your mind.

The second step is to organize the pieces for each segment of your succession plan. When you think about ownership succession, you naturally think about family members, but you also need to think about key employees and what you might want to do to reward them, both now and in anticipation of a change of control. When you think about management succession, you will start with your existing management team. Begin to think about new management you may need and start to think about the leadership skills, interpersonal skills, speaking skills, and other attributes of a CEO you might not have considered when evaluating your current management team. Flesh out your ideas about equity rewards and cash rewards. Think about deferred compensation plans and whether they make sense for you and your business.

Thirdly, as you start to go through this process, use the questionnaire in the appendix to guide you through the various sets of questions and issues. Don't think of this questionnaire as any kind of rigid "bible." You may think of questions that I haven't included, and that's fine.

As your thoughts begin to crystallize, create an outline of bullet points or major issues that you feel need to be addressed. Then begin discussing the topics with your advisors, the people you trust the most. Find out which of your colleagues have gone through this same analysis. Sit down with them and discuss their questions and concerns, as well as your own.

Slowly but surely, the pieces will begin to fit together. I am certain of one thing. If you take the time to march down the road of succession planning, you will learn more about your business—and especially more about your key employees, if not your family members—than you ever knew before. Hopefully, most of that new information will be positive and inspiring to you, but whether it is good news or bad news, you will be more enlightened and more conscious of the key decisions you need to make as the owner about the future of your company and the legacy you want to leave. That alone is worth the effort. The more likely result, however, is that in addition to that realization, you will be able to stitch together a cohesive succession plan that will assure the cementing of that legacy and give you the joy and thrill of knowing that your precious company is in good hands.

Owner Questionnaire
Regarding Succession Planning

1. When do you plan to step down as company CEO?

    ____ 5 years ____ 10 years ____ never ____ other

2. Do you have a succession plan?

    ____ yes ____ no

3. If you answered "yes" to No. 2, when was it last updated or revised?

    ____ within the past year ____ within the past 3 years ____ never

4. If you have a succession plan, who was involved in its creation?

    ____ board of directors ____ other senior management
    ____ other (please specify)

    _____

    _____

5. Have you already selected a successor CEO?

    ____ yes ____ no

6. If you answered "yes" to No. 5, do you plan to transfer ownership of the company to your successor?

____ yes ____ not yet ____ never

7. If you answered "yes" to No. 6, would you plan to transfer ownership all at once or over time?

____ all at once ____ over 3 years ____ over 5 years ____ other

_____

_____

8. Which of the following criteria do you consider most important in a successor? Pick no more than five.

___ Seniority
___ Knowledge of the business
___ Interpersonal skills
___ Business Development
___ Leadership skills
___ Speaking skills
___ Integrity
___ Trust
___ Age
___ Public speaking
___ Common sense
___ Sense of humor
___ "Street smarts"
___ Intelligence
___ Education
___ Other (please specify)

_____

_____

9. Have you discussed succession planning with your senior management?

___ yes ___ no

10. If you have not selected a successor, would you prefer that your successor be chosen from current management, or be an outside selection?

___ current management   ___ outside selection

11. Have you created a plan to transfer ownership to family members as part of your estate plan?

___ yes ___ no

12. If you answered "yes" to No. 11, would you still create a significant equity ownership position for your successor?

___ yes ___ no

13. If you answered "yes" to No. 12, have you developed a plan to accomplish this goal?

___ yes ___ no

14. If your lenders, vendors, suppliers, or customers have asked you about succession, what has been your typical response?

_____

_____

15. Have you planned for succession in an emergency?

___ yes ___ no

16. Have you given equity to your children or spouse?

____ yes   ____ no

17. If you answered "yes" to No. 16, have you provided for what happens in the event of the donee's death or divorce?

____ yes   ____ no

18. If and when a successor is selected, what is the most important advice you would like to give him or her?

_____

_____

19. What is your strongest objection to developing an effective succession plan?

____ diversion of time   ____ cost   ____ I'm just not ready
____ other

_____

_____

20. Have you unsuccessfully tried to develop a succession plan?

____ yes   ____ no

21. What were the main reasons that your earlier efforts did not succeed?

_____

_____